Celebrations

AT THE
COUNTRY HOUSE

21 20 19 18 17   5 4 3 2 1

Copyright © 2017 Carolyn Westbrook
Photographs © 2017 April Pizana, except
pages 6, 13, 19, 175 © 2017 Carolyn Westbrook

Published by
Gibbs Smith
P.O. Box 667
Layton, Utah 84041

1.800.835.4993 orders
www.gibbs-smith.com

Designed by Aimee Contois/LemonAid Factory
Produced by Virginia Brimhall Snow

Printed and bound in Hong Kong

Gibbs Smith books are printed on either recycled, 100% post-consumer waste,
FSC-certified papers or on paper produced from sustainable PEFC-certified
forest/controlled wood source. Learn more at www.pefc.org.
Library of Congress Cataloging-in-Publication Data

Names: Westbrook, Carolyn, author.
Title: Celebrations at the country house / Carolyn Westbrook ;
photographs by
  April Pizana.
Description: First edition. | Layton, Utah : Gibbs Smith, [2017] |
Includes
  index.
Identifiers: LCCN 2017003903 | ISBN 9781423645771 (hardcover)
Subjects: LCSH: Cooking, American--Southern style. | Cooking--Texas. |
  Seasonal cooking. | Entertaining. | LCGFT: Cookbooks.
Classification: LCC TX715.2.S68 W4584 2017 | DDC 641.5975--dc23
LC record available at https://lccn.loc.gov/2017003903

Carolyn Westbrook

Celebrations
AT THE
COUNTRY HOUSE

PHOTOGRAPHS BY APRIL PIZANA

GIBBS SMITH
TO ENRICH AND INSPIRE HUMANKIND

Contents

Introduction: 7

Spring

Southern Brunch: 17

Scratch Buttermilk Biscuits • Country Sausage Gravy • Cheesy Scrambled Eggs Florentine • Texas Pecan Praline Muffins • Bacon-Jalapeño Cheesy Grits • Texas Fencerow Blackberry Preserves • Strawberry Preserves

Tex~Mex gathering: 35

Shrimp Ceviche • Homemade Guacamole • Nick's Favorite Fresh Salsa • Aunt Kim's Cheesy Spanish Rice • Spicy Stuffed Cornbread • Southwestern Squash Casserole

Sunday Dinner After Church: 47

Nana's Famous Fried Chicken • Texas's-Best Fried Green Tomatoes • Cornbread • Family-Favorite Macaroni and Cheese • Black-Eyed Peas with Snaps • Tomato, Cucumber, and Feta Salad • Peach Cobbler

Ladies Day Luncheon: 63

Cranberry Chicken Salad • Pimento Cheese-Stuffed Celery • Classic Cucumber Sandwiches • Lime Sherbet Punch • Coconut Cake

Summer

Fourth of July Barbeque: 81

Easy Barbeque Ribs • Aunty Lou's Brisket • Southern Mashed Potato Salad • Mexican Cole Slaw • Deviled Eggs • Sugar-Free Cherry Pie

Celebrate Charlotte: 95

Sherry's Famous Beer Cheese Dip • Caesar Salad with Homemade Dressing • Carolyn's Best Lasagna • Pasta with Garden-Fresh Tomato Sauce • Uncle Chad's Tomato Caprese Salad • Chicken with Goat Cheese • Aunt Karen's Spaghetti • Parmesan Garlic Toast • Strawberry Champagne Punch • Grandmother's Fudge Cake • Strawberry Layer Cake

Fish Fry and Fish Favorites: 119

Hush Puppies • Cole Slaw • Fried Catfish • Almond-Crusted Salmon with Spring Greens and Blue Cheese • Southern Salmon Patties • Dad's Fish Dipping Sauce • Green Tomato Relish • Spicy Garlic Pickles

Sandwiches: 131

Simply Perfect Shrimp BLT • Fried Baloney and Egg Sandwich

Autumn

Soup for Supper: 141
Down-Home Chicken and Dumplings • Broccoli and Cheese Soup • Nick's Cheeseburger in a Bowl Soup • Blue Ribbon Beef Stew

Autumn Dinner Al Fresco: 153
Chicken Pot Pie

Halloween Barn Party: 157
Venison Chili • Cheesy Spinach and Orange Pepper Dip • White Chili with Chicken • Nana's Bean Salad • Chocolate-Dipped Apples • Gummy Worm Pudding Cups

Meatloaf Monday: 171
Barbeque Meatloaf • Loaded Buttermilk Mashed Potatoes • Fried Okra • Tim's Favorite Pound Cake • Cream Cheese Spinach

Winter

Chinese Non~Take~Out Dinner : 183
Orange Chicken • Fried Rice

The Night Before Christmas : 187
Spicy Rosemary and Black Pepper Cashews • Layered Salad • Stuffed Turkey Breast • Holiday Dressing • Cranberry Relish • Jalapeño Corn Casserole • Sugar-Free Pecan Pie

Food for Thought: 202
Herb Bouquets • Carolyn's Tips for Decorating Tables

Index: 206

Introduction

Life has a way of turning out the way it should, I think. It's funny how the things that influence us growing up make for the melting pot of our personalities. I was born into the world of design; with my mama being a designer and artist, she would drag me around the city to every antique market and would spend endless hours choosing fabrics. I didn't have a playhouse, but I would decorate my friend's playhouse and then redecorate it. I remember cooking on her toy stove and getting in trouble for filling the play sink with water to wash the dishes. I am fortunate that my childhood was filled with memories of not only decorating but cooking, entertaining, growing, gardening, and gathering around the supper table.

I spent summers, holidays, and many weekends at my grandparents' farm. I was born and raised in Texas, and they lived in a tiny Texas town where the white rock dust swirled at least once or twice a day as a car would pass down their back-country road. That was back when everyone waved at each other as they passed, and you never met a stranger—if you did, by the time they stopped for a Coke at the local store, everyone in town would know their business. Some of my favorite memories are of the gatherings that we had there because of the homegrown and homemade food that my grandmother, Mutty, would make. I am reminded of our Carolyn Westbrook Home mantra that says it perfectly: "Creating a Home that Reflects the Spirit of You."™ Everyone's home is as different as their personality and history, and our homes are a reflection of who we are. That includes the food we serve and the smells that drift through the house from the pot on the stove.

Twenty something years ago when my husband, Joe, and I started our family, I wanted our children to know the country life that I had known. I saw an ad in the Dallas paper one day for a historic home on twenty-five acres that included a pear and apricot orchard. Never mind that I was not quite finished with a renovation on a ranch-style home in the city. The ad was only in the paper that one day and we were not even looking for a home, but off we went. Some might say it was fate, my husband might have thought differently at the time. We pulled up to a dilapidated, old rambling house, and Joe thought that I had lost my mind as I walked through it talking of restoring the enormous falling-down structure with peeling paint, no air-conditioning, and a bowing roof. The apricot and pear orchard turned out to be a few scrawny trees in desperate need of water. This was at a time before renovating was popular, and our big ol' contractor said it best when he told me that it would be cheaper to tear it down and start over. I was determined to raise my children in the country. I could see past all of the rotted wood and what were then desert-like surroundings to a beautiful country house surrounded by gardens that were overflowing with squash, fresh tomatoes, and okra that I would serve for supper. So a few weeks later, we drove off with the big city in our rearview mirror to begin the romance with our country house.

Moving to the country, you begin to slow down. You leave the whine of the asphalt for the sound of a gravel road that crunches beneath your tires as you pull onto the farm market road. You cannot help but be captivated by the changing of the seasons here at our country house. Not only does the decor change with the season, but so do our menus. This is a place where in the summer you can kick off your shoes and feel the coolness of the green grass between your toes. It is a place where you cannot wait to plow the earth as soon as the last frost is over so that you can get the garden started. I remember my grandfather, Papa, who would always rise before dawn and wore overalls every day of his life except on Sundays, when he went to church. He would have coffee at the table every morning while Mutty cooked up biscuits, sausage gravy, and fresh eggs that had been gathered from the chicken house.

We now have a country house and beautiful gardens that deliver a bountiful harvest. Here recipes are passed down and passed around the table through the generations, written down on scraps of paper or old recipe cards in handwriting that is sometimes a bit hard to read for the smudging and smears of vanilla extract or tomato sauce over the years. This book is a collection of those tried-and-true recipes that hold food memories of the beloved people who made them and the delicious meals we shared.

Our country house has come a long way, but it is always a work in progress. The house and grounds are never really done, for each season brings about change. In spring, the trees start to bud out in all of their glorious greenery, the hydrangeas begin to bloom, and the greens and onions start coming in. Summer offers everything under the sun, including big, juicy homegrown tomatoes that I adore for breakfast on a slice of wheat toast, sprinkled with a bit of salt—even better with a fried egg that has just been plucked from the chicken house on top. Then after you think you are tired of the heat, the first cool breeze of autumn blows in and soon the pumpkins are ready to be carved—it is time for the annual Halloween party and hayride. The cooler weather brings on hearty meals like beef stew, and everyone knows my love of soup—almost any kind.

Before we know it, Christmas is coming with our Night Before Christmas dinner. Just after the Christmas Eve service has ended, and we go out into the cold night air and back down the farm market road to the country house, we are excited about what awaits. As we open the back door, we feel the warmth coming from within, and the smells wafting from the oven suddenly become more important than the presents under the tree. As I pop rolls into the oven and we light the candles on the Christmas Eve table, everyone gathers around and can hardly wait until the food is on the table and thanks is given for all of the blessings of the season.

Moving to this small Texas town was like going back in time, with Family Night at the community center and the Pot Luck Sunday Dinner that happens once a month after church; you see, here in the South, dinner is lunch and supper is dinner. Sort of confusing if you're not used to the southern small-town way of life, and let's not forget the Annual Fish Fry or the Ice Cream Social. Any excuse for everyone to gather, eat, and visit, that's what we do. I hope that my recipes and ways of cooking will inspire those of you who have not experienced growing your own vegetables or cooking a whole meal from scratch. There is really nothing to it. I am a cook, not a chef; I do it out of necessity, just as generations before me have done, and you can too. It is essential to feel comfortable and confident in the kitchen and not be afraid to try something new. Cooking is kind of like decorating: you keep adding and mixing until the taste is just right. There is pleasure in serving a home-cooked meal with real plates and utensils.

I wanted this cookbook to be filled not only with glorious photography and food but with my love for decorating and entertaining as well. Here is a celebration of all of the seasons and the food that we bring to the table for our family, served in a beautiful way. Everyone who knows me knows that I always say "It's always a good time for a party," and I love having a get-together to look forward to. That is really what life is all about—family, gathering, and the cooking that gives us a great excuse to do that. I do love any sort of decorating, so whether it is a tablescape of a full-blown soirée, count me in.

We have always gathered around the supper table with our family and blessed the food before we eat. When it comes to home and family, these are the moments that our family and friends will remember. I hope that you enjoy this book, use the recipes often, and throw an impromptu party just as an excuse to get together. Remember, there is no place like home, and that is where the real memories are made.

"Creating a Home that Reflects the Spirit of You."™ What could be more beautiful?

xoxo,
Carolyn

Southern Brunch   17

Tex~Mex Gathering   35

Sunday Dinner After Church   47

Ladies Day Luncheon   63

Spring

ho doesn't love spring? After months of cold weather with your nose pressed against the freezing window, waiting for sunshine and green grass, it is finally here. For me, spring is always a time for new beginnings and excitement about what the new year will bring. It is a time of rebirth and beauty as the leaves begin budding on the trees and the bright yellow daffodils and tulips bloom in the front garden. It is also a time to refresh the house and the earth, as we till the earth for the garden. Plants and seeds are planted in the newly tilled earth for a spring and summer filled with squash, tomatoes, cucumbers, onions, peppers, okra, and everything else that we love. These will make the delicious pickles, salads, soups and main dishes for the year. We plant marigolds to keep away garden pests, and zinnias and sunflowers for impromptu bouquets.

There is something great about being able to grow your own food and then pick it, and serve it to your family. It doesn't get much fresher than that—farm to table.

We know what is in the food that we eat. We do not use pesticides and we try to garden organically. After tilling the land, which is my son Nicholas's job, we begin spreading the cottonseed meal. We get ours at the feed store, and it really helps the garden to thrive. Then we lay the black garden cloth down and pin it to the ground to deter the weeds. Then section by section we plant the garden.

You do not have to live in the country to have a garden. Raised garden beds are wonderful for a suburban yard, or a container garden can yield some great things on an apartment balcony. I hope some of our favorite recipes here on the farm will inspire you to have a garden of your own.

Our menus change seasonally, and in the spring season we are all about getting outside after a long winter of cold and rain. We are fortunate to have a huge front porch at our country house that offers plenty of seating, so that we can sit out there to eat a meal or to gather at night to watch the stars. This book features our Southern Brunch, because every weekend here is full of sausage gravy and biscuits, homemade preserves, and our jalapeño cheesy grits. From there we invite you to our Sunday Dinner After Church, which is filled with our favorite fried chicken, cornbread, and peach cobbler. And who wouldn't enjoy the Ladies Garden Club Luncheon, which is a nostalgic treat of lime sherbet punch along with fancy crust-less cucumber sandwiches, which I adore. There are plenty of recipes in between, and they are sure to make you look forward to spring more than ever.

SOUTHERN BRUNCH

Scratch Buttermilk Biscuits   20

Country Sausage Gravy   23

Cheesy Scrambled Eggs Florentine   24

Texas Pecan Praline Muffins   26

Bacon~Jalapeño Cheesy Grits   27

Texas Fencerow Blackberry Preserves   31

Strawberry Preserves   32

*H*aving grown up in Texas, I might know a thing or two about brunch and garden club parties. My mama would occasionally take me along to one of her ladies parties if I was on my best behavior, or every now and then she would host the event. Lordy, y'all, that was a big deal if the ladies were coming to our house for the party. My mother was a noted designer in her day and an artist. She was president of the PTA and in the art club and garden club, so there was always some kind of affair going on.

Mama and her best friend, Donna, took me with them to my first brunch when I was a small child. I wore one of my fanciest dresses, and as we pulled up to the house, I could see past the window boxes and through the blue-and-white gingham curtains to all of the busy goings-on inside. I remember stepping into one of the prettiest settings that I had ever seen with all of this amazing food that was being served on Blue Italian Spode dishes. I was captivated by these ladies all in their dresses and pearls. More than that, I mostly remember the cozy setting on this spring day and the scrumptious food that was plated on the beautiful plates that went perfectly with the blue gingham curtains. I had cherry cheesecake for the first time and still remember how good it tasted.

That day began my love affair with blue transferware. I've searched many a box and table at flea markets looking for additions to my collection. I have several

different patterns, but I treasure most the Spode that reminds me of the party.

Blue-and-white is absolutely perfect for a country house and a country fried

chicken dinner.

Here's to a good, old-fashioned Southern Brunch!

Scratch Buttermilk Biscuits

In Texas, biscuits and gravy is a staple, and it's one of my son Nick's favorite foods. My best friend's mom, Mimi, used to tell me that she would rather whoop up a batch of biscuits than crack a can. She could whip out a breakfast for eight or ten and make it look like it was easy. My Mutty could do the same. Boy, did we kids love going to Mutty and Papa's house, because there was always a big breakfast with biscuits that were slathered with butter and homemade pear preserves. Ooh-wee, it doesn't get any better than that.

Here is my grandma's biscuit recipe, and her tips were this: always sift your dry ingredients, and don't roll the dough, just pat it out. For goodness' sake, don't handle the dough too much or the biscuits will be tough, and always use a cast iron skillet.

Makes 12 biscuits

3 cups all-purpose flour

1 teaspoon salt

1 teaspoon baking soda

2 teaspoons baking powder

1 1/2 sticks chilled salted butter, cut into small slices

1/4 stick butter for melting in skillet

1 cup buttermilk

Preheat oven to 425 degrees. In a large bowl, sift the dry ingredients together using a sifter. Add slices of butter and work those into the dry ingredients with a fork until the butter is totally combined with flour.

Melt the other 1/4 stick of butter in a cast iron skillet on the stovetop and spread it all over the bottom of the skillet; then remove from heat.

Add buttermilk to the flour mixture and combine thoroughly until a dough forms. If the dough is too dry, add a tiny bit of milk until it gets to the right consistency. If it is too wet, then add a tiny bit of flour until it is right. Place a tablespoon of flour on the countertop or board and pat the biscuit dough out into a large round. Use a round biscuit cutter to cut the biscuits. Once cut, take one round of biscuit dough and swipe it in the melted butter, top and bottom. Then set the biscuit in the skillet. Repeat with other biscuit rounds. When the pan is full, place it in the oven and cook until golden brown, about 15 minutes.

Country Sausage Gravy

Biscuits and gravy is the epitome of southern comfort food. You can make this recipe with sausage, or just make a plain white country gravy that is also good on mashed potatoes and chicken fried steak. Let's face it: I have been known to just eat it out of the pan— of course, that's called tasting. The cook must always taste the food. Gravy can be tricky and this is the way my grandma made it.

My friend Debbie and I always cooked, and our kids went to school together. My daughter Alex came home from a sleepover at Meg's one day and informed me that Debbie made better gravy than I did. Those are fightin' words, and I had to go over there one Sunday and see for myself. As the gravy bubbled on the stove, she explained to me that you just gotta get a good scald on it, and she was right. After her tutorial, I agree. The flour has to get a good scald to get it cooked, and the gravy gets a little brown. This stuff is great right out of the pan, but it's scrumptious over a homemade buttermilk biscuit.

Makes 3 cups

1/4 cup canola oil

1/4 cup sausage drippings*

3/4 cup all-purpose flour

1/2 cup canned evaporated milk

2 1/2 cups whole milk

1 teaspoon salt

1 teaspoon black pepper

1 pound sausage, fully cooked and crumbled

Heat the canola oil and sausage drippings in a large cast iron skillet on medium-high heat. Add flour and begin whisking as soon as it hits the pan; you do not want to burn the flour. Stir until the two are combined and keep stirring the flour until it is browned, but be careful not to burn. Add all the milk at one time and continue whisking to keep lumps from forming. Leave the gravy on the stove to bubble and thicken, stirring constantly. Add salt and pepper. As gravy thickens, reduce the heat. Once it is to your desired consistency, remove from heat and stir in the sausage.

*(If you don't have sausage drippings, then add 1/4 cup more canola oil.

Tip: Use a whisk for the gravy; it is much better for preventing lumps in your gravy.

Cheesy Scrambled Eggs Florentine

When my kids would have friends over, they always wanted cheesy eggs. That's what we called them. Alex now always wants spinach in her eggs, and that is my favorite too. One of the great things about living in the country is being able to go out to the chicken house and grab your eggs: we have Araucana hens, which lay the most beautiful pastel green eggs. I love to have breakfast for dinner, and there has been many a night that we have feasted on these eggs. Cheesy goodness comes from a hunk of Velveeta, which has become a luxury with the prices of this cheese-like product skyrocketing. "What makes it so expensive?" I ask myself as I stand in the grocery aisle debating over whether to splurge for the big box or go for the smaller one. I usually grab the bigger one, rationalizing that I don't think it goes bad and it is really the only thing for some of my casserole and soup recipes, so I will live a little . . . LOL.

Makes 4 servings

8 eggs

1 cup chopped fresh spinach

1/4 cup chopped green onion

4 slices cooked bacon, crumbled

4 (1/4-inch) slices Velveeta

2 tablespoons butter

Salt and pepper

Crack the eggs into a large bowl and whisk until smooth. Add the spinach, onion, bacon, and Velveeta. Melt the butter in a skillet over low heat. Raise the temperature to medium and add the egg mixture. Stir to avoid sticking until the eggs reach desired consistency. Remove from the heat and put a lid on the skillet so Velveeta can melt thoroughly. Add salt and pepper to taste. Serve immediately.

Texas Pecan Praline Muffins

Everyone at Bible study raves about this recipe. It yields 12 mini-muffins. We usually double the recipe, but they are very rich, so you do not need much.

Makes 12 mini muffins

2 eggs

¹/₂ cup flour

1 cup lightly packed brown sugar

¹/₂ cup melted butter

1 tablespoon vanilla

1 cup chopped pecans

Bacon-Jalapeño Cheesy Grits

Any good southerner has to cook grits— it's kind of a rite of passage before they will let you past the Mason-Dixon line. I grew up eating grits with butter and salt, and I always had a taste for them. I ate them on vacation at a big southern mansion in Vicksburg when I was much younger, and that was where they served cheesy grits for breakfast. Well, we thought we had died and gone to heaven. I decided to do mine up a little bit more over the years by adding crispy bacon and the spice of jalapeño. After all, bacon makes anything better, and if you live in Texas then bring on the heat. These grits are not just for breakfast. They make a great side dish for any entrée. Even if you are sitting there thinking that you don't like grits, I bet these will change your mind.

Makes 6 servings

2 cups grits

6 cups water

1 stick butter

1/2 teaspoon garlic powder

1/4 cup evaporated milk

6 strips crispy bacon, chopped

2 1/2 cups Colby-Jack cheese, divided

2 pickled jalapeños, finely chopped

2 green onions, finely chopped

Salt and pepper

Heat the oven to 350 degrees. Cook the grits in water according to package directions. Add the butter, garlic powder, and milk to grits and mix. Add in the bacon, 1 1/2 cups cheese, jalapeños, and green onions and combine thoroughly. Add salt and pepper to taste. Transfer grits to a baking dish and top with remaining cheese. Bake until cheese is bubbly.

SPRING

Texas Fencerow Blackberry Preserves

Here in Texas, we cannot wait until the blackberries ripen in the spring. There is a fencerow that is our favorite blackberry picking spot. Nick spotted them this year and told me to hurry up and get over there if I wanted to get some blackberries because the birds were eating them all up. I pulled on my rubber boots, which are necessary gear when gathering blackberries because there are often snakes in the fencerow where the berries are. The dew was still fresh on the berries as the sun was just rising in the sky. The birds fluttered about in the trees overhead as I arrived with my bucket, as if to tell me that those berries were for them. The berries were plump and I just couldn't resist plucking one off the vine for a taste. It was sweet and juicy, not like the ones that you buy in the store that are often sour. I filled up my bucket thinking of the cobbler and jelly that I would make. My daughter Victoria has always loved blackberry cobbler, ever since she was old enough to eat. Blackberry season doesn't last long, so if you know where there's a fencerow of berries, you'd better get some before the birds eat them all.

Makes 3 1/2 pints

4 cups blackberries, rinsed and dried

1/4 cup lemon juice

7 1/2 cups sugar

2 pouches liquid fruit pectin

1/2 teaspoon butter

Place berries in a large pot on medium heat and mash berries to extract the juice. Add lemon juice and sugar, stirring constantly. Turn up the heat and bring to a boil. Add fruit pectin and butter (the butter helps discourage foaming and thereby prevents boilovers). Boil for exactly 1 minute then skim any foam off of mixture with a metal spoon (its thin, sharp edge is good for skimming foam). Remove from heat. The jam is ready to can. Follow proper canning instructions, which can be found in the fruit pectin box or canning books.

Strawberry Preserves

There is nothing better than homemade preserves. My grandmother had a real root cellar, which was basically a large hole in the ground with a door on it and you could see the tree roots coming through the walls, hence the name root cellar. There were shelves lined with pickled beets, chow-chow, and of course preserves. Most jellies, jams, and preserves that you buy at the store nowadays contain high fructose corn syrup and the fruit is barely visible. I like big chunks of fruit that I can actually taste. I had always thought that canning was an all-day process, but it isn't. I did my first round of canning in my twenties, and it is not that hard at all. It is something that you can easily do and oh-my-gosh is it worth it. I would recommend that you get a little canning funnel that helps when you are spooning the jam into jars. Also, a pair of tongs is handy for lifting the lids and jars out of the boiling water. I have a system now that I do because I have canned a lot over the years. I put a cookie sheet next to the stovetop to place the jars on when they come out of the hot bath. Just follow the directions below and you will be in for a sweet treat.

Makes 3 1/2 pints

4 cups strawberries, washed and sliced

7 cups sugar

1 tablespoon lemon juice

1 pouch liquid fruit pectin

1 teaspoon butter

Place strawberries in a stockpot over medium heat. I use a potato masher to mash them a bit but leave them chunky. Add sugar and lemon juice to strawberries and combine. Bring mixture to a boil, stirring constantly. Add fruit pectin and continue to stir. Add butter to prevent foaming. Keep boiling for 1 minute, stirring constantly. Skim off any foam with a metal spoon. Take the pot off of the heat. Follow the instructions from the fruit pectin box for the proper canning procedure.

TEX-MEX GATHERING

Shrimp Ceviche   36

Homemade Guacamole   38

Nick's Favorite Fresh Salsa   41

Aunt Kim's Cheesy Spanish Rice   42

Spicy Stuffed Cornbread   44

Southwestern Squash Casserole   45

Shrimp Ceviche

My mama has been making this recipe for years. My daddy loves shrimp, and ceviche tastes so fresh on a hot summer day. I love to eat it with tortilla chips.

Makes about 3 cups

1 1/2 pounds frozen cleaned, deveined, pre-cooked extra small shrimp

Juice of 2 limes, divided

1 red onion, finely chopped

2 red tomatoes, chopped

4 tablespoons finely chopped cilantro

2 jalapeños, seeded, deveined, and finely chopped

1 tablespoon pickled jalapeño juice

2 tablespoons extra virgin olive oil

2 tablespoons salt

Cracked black pepper

2 avocados, cut into small cubes

Cilantro sprigs, for garnish

Place the shrimp in a colander and rinse with cold water to thaw. Drain shrimp and place in a bowl. Add half the lime juice to the shrimp. Add red onion, tomatoes, cilantro, jalapeños, jalapeño juice, olive oil, salt, and pepper to taste. Let marinate in the refrigerator for 30 minutes. Drizzle remaining lime juice over the avocado and add avocado to the bowl. Mix, garnish with cilantro sprigs, and serve.

Homemade Guacamole

Some people do not care for the color or consistency of guacamole. As my dad would say, "Great! There's more for the rest of us." This guacamole recipe is simple, super fresh, and delicious. We love to use it on top of a salad, in tacos or fajitas, or just to eat right out of the bowl with a bag of tortilla chips. Yum!

Makes about 3 cups

4 ripe avocados, peeled and chopped

2 tomatoes, diced

1 small onion, finely chopped

2 tablespoons pickled jalapeño juice

Juice of 1 lime

Salt and pepper

Fresh cilantro, finely chopped, optional

Mash the avocados until smooth in a large bowl. Add the tomatoes, onion, jalapeño juice, and lime juice; season with salt and pepper to taste and add cilantro as desired. Stir everything together, leaving it chunky. That's all there is; it's ready to eat.

Nick's Favorite Fresh Salsa

My love affair with Tex-Mex started long before my favorite son-in-law, Jose Luis, entered into our lives, although he has introduced me to some pretty delicious recipes. It really began when I was a child on my first trip to El Fenix in Dallas, which is a Mexican restaurant that has flourished over the years. Back then, we rarely ate out and this was our first encounter with enchiladas and chiles rellenos, and their salsa was amazing. It was an all-you-can-eat buffet, and my brothers would get downright embarrassing; therefore, the need to make Tex-Mex fare at home was born. We feel that we have perfected the recipe for salsa, but everyone's taste varies. I happen to love cilantro, but if you do not care for it, leave it out. My son could drink this out of a bowl; we have to watch him, or he will take the entire batch to his room and leave a tiny bowl for everybody else!

Makes about 4 cups

2 tablespoons canola oil

2 cloves garlic

Handful of chopped fresh cilantro

1 teaspoon salt

1 teaspoon garlic powder

Juice of 1 large lime

1 (28-ounce) can diced tomatoes

2 tablespoons pickled jalapeño juice

2 pickled jalapeños, finely chopped

Tortilla chips, for serving

Place the oil in a food processor and add the garlic. Process until garlic is finely chopped. Add the cilantro, salt, garlic powder, lime juice, tomatoes, jalapeño juice, and jalapeños; process until well mixed and the consistency of salsa. Serve with tortilla chips.

Aunt Kim's Cheesy Spanish Rice

This was my best friend Kim's favorite recipe and one of my favorites too. It goes great with Spinach and Kale Salad (xx) or a pot of beans. Of course, everything is better with cheese on top, and this recipe does not disappoint.

Makes about 12 servings

8 slices bacon

1 onion, chopped

2 cloves garlic, minced

1 (28~ounce) can diced tomatoes

1 teaspoon cumin

1/2 teaspoon garlic powder

1 teaspoon salt

1/2 teaspoon black pepper

4 cups cooked rice

2 cups grated cheddar cheese or Monterey Jack

Preheat the oven to 350 degrees.

Fry bacon in a large skillet until crisp. Remove bacon, drain, and chop. Leave bacon drippings in the skillet and add onion and garlic. Sauté until soft. Add tomatoes, bacon, cumin, garlic powder, salt, and pepper; mix well and simmer for a few minutes, until heated through. Place cooked rice in a large bowl and add the tomato mixture, mixing thoroughly. Taste to make sure that the salt and pepper are to your liking. Pour into a large casserole dish and top with cheese. Bake until cheese is golden and bubbly, about 20 minutes.

Spicy Stuffed Cornbread

This is a traditional southern cornbread with a bit of a Mexican twist. It is hearty enough for a one-dish meal and is sure to become a favorite.

Makes 8 servings

2 (8.5-ounce) boxes Jiffy Cornbread Mix

2 eggs

²/₃ cup buttermilk

1 (14.75-ounce) can cream-style corn

4 pickled jalapeños, minced

1 ¹/₂ pounds ground beef

1 (1.25-ounce) package taco seasoning

¹/₂ teaspoon garlic powder

1 onion, chopped

2 tablespoons butter

2 cups grated Colby Jack cheese, divided

Preheat the oven to 400 degrees.

Prepare the cornbread batter in a large bowl according to package directions using the eggs and buttermilk (instead of milk). Add the corn and jalapeños and stir.

Cook meat over medium-high heat until browned and then drain. Add the seasoning pack and garlic powder and combine. Add onion and sauté until it is soft.

Heat the butter in a large cast iron skillet. Once melted, add half of the cornbread batter into the skillet. Add the meat mixture and sprinkle with 1 cup of the cheese. Pour remaining cornbread batter on top of the meat mixture and top with remaining 1 cup cheese. Bake for approximately 25 minutes, or until cornbread is golden and a toothpick inserted in the center comes out clean.

Southwestern Squash Casserole

My mama came up with this recipe years ago, and it is unlike any squash casserole that I have ever had. It tastes just like enchiladas—without the meat. At every potluck we have taken this to over the years, people have wanted the recipe—so here it is.

Makes 6 servings

2 pounds summer squash (a combination of yellow and zucchini), sliced, boiled, and drained

2 cups crushed corn tortilla chips

1 (10.75-ounce) can cream of chicken soup

1 (10.75-ounce) can cream of mushroom soup

1 (4.5-ounce) can chopped green chiles

1 onion, chopped

1 large egg, beaten

2 teaspoons cumin

2 teaspoons garlic powder

1 cup melted Velveeta

1 cup grated Colby Jack cheese

Preheat the oven to 400 degrees. Prepare a 9 x 13-inch baking dish with nonstick cooking spray.

Take the cooled, drained squash and blot dry with a paper towel. Place in a bowl. Add the tortilla chips, cream of chicken and cream of mushroom soups, chiles, onion, egg, cumin, garlic powder, and Velveeta and combine. Transfer mixture to the baking dish and top with Colby Jack. Bake until golden and bubbly, about 30 minutes.

SUNDAY DINNER AFTER CHURCH

Nana's Famous Fried Chicken   50

Texas's-Best Fried Green Tomatoes   52

Cornbread   55

Family-Favorite Macaroni and Cheese   56

Black-Eyed Peas with Snaps   59

Tomato, Cucumber, and Feta Salad   60

Peach Cobbler   61

There has always been Sunday dinner after church. It's something that everyone looks forward to because it is now one of the few times when the entire family gets together around the table. I remember sitting in church as a child, impatiently kicking the pew in front of me, thinking of lunch, and I would get the evil eye from Mama. I would instantly freeze because that look meant that you were in for it.

I could hardly wait until the chicken was fried, which seemed to take forever. My grandmother's tip for the best fried chicken was this: always cook low and slow so that it doesn't burn on the outside and remain raw on the inside. Use a cast iron skillet and Crisco. It's gotta be Crisco to get that good crunchy, flaky crust. My mama makes boneless fried chicken breasts, and they are delicious, but I argue with her that it is not fried chicken unless it is on the bone.

Here, I offer a glimpse of our own Sunday dinner after church—fried chicken, macaroni and cheese, fresh-picked black-eyed peas, cornbread, and tomato-cucumber salad. For dessert, it's homemade peach cobbler—and what could be better than that? This meal brings out the Southerner in everyone.

Y'all will be saying "Bless your heart" in no time!

Nana's Famous Fried Chicken

This recipe is a family favorite that has been passed down since the days when my great grandmother was going out to the coop to get the chicken. (Our chickens are like our pets, so I cannot imagine that. I do like my mama did when she would just head on down to the Busy Bee grocery to get her chicken.) My grandmother cooked up chicken every Sunday, and Papa loved inviting people in to eat, so the house was always full of good food and a lot of laughter. My grandmother's tips and the recipe below result in the perfect piece of fried chicken.

Makes 4 to 6 servings

2 cups buttermilk

2 cups all-purpose flour

1 teaspoon salt

1 teaspoon black pepper

1/2 teaspoon garlic powder

1/2 teaspoon paprika

1/4 teaspoon cayenne pepper

1 fryer chicken, cut into pieces

2 sticks (2 cups) Crisco

Place the buttermilk in a bowl. In another bowl, combine the flour, salt, pepper, garlic powder, paprika, and cayenne pepper. Soak the chicken in the buttermilk and then dredge in the flour mixture; repeat.

Place the Crisco into a medium cast iron skillet and heat over medium heat until bubbly. Place chicken into the skillet without crowding. Cook 3 to 4 pieces at a time and wait for the crust to set up on one side before turning. Remember to fry the chicken low and slow, turning the heat down a couple of notches below medium heat. Fry for about 25 minutes total, until chicken is done in the center. Test by piercing the chicken piece in the center to make sure it is cooked all the way through. Remove from skillet and place chicken on paper towels to drain.

SPRING

51

Texas's-Best Fried Green Tomatoes

My family waits for the first tomato to come in like we're kids with our noses pressed against the glass at the candy store. Once the ground has been plowed, we always debate on what the best variety of tomato is. My daddy likes Celebrity, while I like Big Boy. My brother Chad grows thousands of Sweet 100s. I tell him that those are not the best, because you cannot cut a big slab to fry up for fried green tomatoes or put them on a piece of toast. My mama likes the golden heirloom tomatoes, and I am not gonna lie, there are years where they are absolutely the best tasting.

I stand out in the garden looking at the ground to see what is coming up. It's like the anticipation of Christmas morning when I see a little green sprout . . . success. (That is, if the grasshoppers and bunnies will leave everything alone.) The first tomato is always the most delicious, and as I go out to water the garden in the morning and spy my first couple of green tomatoes. I pluck them and practically run back to the house to grab the cornmeal and the cast iron skillet. Today there will be fried green tomatoes.

Makes 16 slices

1 cup canola oil

3–4 green tomatoes, sliced 1/2 inch thick

1 cup buttermilk

1 cup cornmeal

Salt

Ranch dressing, for serving

Heat the oil for frying in a 12-inch cast iron skillet on medium heat. Soak the tomatoes in the buttermilk and then cover in cornmeal; repeat the process. Place the green tomatoes into the oil and fry, letting the crust set up on one side before turning. Fry over medium heat until golden and crispy, about 3 to 5 minutes. Remove from the pan and place on a plate lined with paper towels for draining. Salt immediately to taste. I like to serve these with Ranch dressing.

SPRING

Cornbread

Every time I make this cornbread, it is everyone's favorite. I have had people fight for the last piece right here in my kitchen. Once, I took a plate of leftovers with fried chicken, black-eyed-peas, macaroni, and cornbread to our friend, and his comment was that the cornbread was the best that he ever had. Funny, because it is so simple to make. Mutty always used Jiffy cornbread mix and then doctored it up and made it her own. The trick here is to always cook it in a cast iron skillet, and you have to heat a little bit of bacon drippings in that skillet before you pour in the batter. It will sizzle as it hits the pan, and it sort of fries the bottom of the cornbread. Mimi always told me that sweet cornbread was called Johnny cake, while savory cornbread could be anything from buttermilk to hot water cornbread. This is Mutty's version and it has been passed down through the generations here in Texas.

Makes 8–9 servings

2 (8.5-ounce) boxes Jiffy Corn Muffin Mix

2 eggs

2/3 cup milk

1 (14.75-ounce) can cream-style corn

1 cup shredded Colby Jack cheese

2 tablespoons bacon drippings or oil

Heat the oven to 400 degrees. Prepare the cornbread batter in a large bowl according to package directions using the eggs and milk. Stir in the corn and cheese. Heat the bacon drippings in a 12-inch cast iron skillet on medium-high heat until hot. Pour the cornbread mixture into the skillet; it will sizzle. Place the skillet in the oven and bake approximately 25 minutes, until cornbread is golden brown and a toothpick inserted in the center comes out clean.

Family-Favorite
Macaroni and Cheese

When we all get together, everyone is always wanting more of the ooey-gooey deliciousness of our creamy macaroni and cheese. I use the giant elbow macaroni that cradle the cheese and sauce like a baby in its mother's arms. The last time I had the boxed kind at a friend's house, the noodles were so skinny and straight that they looked like a straight pin instead of a noodle; even cooked, they were a disappointment. I like a big, robust noodle that can carry the load of this decadent cheese sauce. We make a roux for our cheesy sauce and then layer the top with shredded cheese. This is the ultimate comfort food.

Makes 8–10 servings

3 cups large elbow macaroni

4 tablespoons butter

3 tablespoons all-purpose flour

2 cups milk

4 ounces cream cheese

3 (1-inch-thick) slices Velveeta

4 ounces shredded mozzarella cheese

1/2 teaspoon salt

2 cups shredded Colby Jack cheese

Preheat the oven to 350 degrees. Prepare a 9 x 13-inch baking dish with nonstick cooking spray.

Cook the macaroni and drain it. Set aside.

In a saucepan, melt the butter and add the flour, whisking continuously. Add milk while continuing to whisk. Keep whisking until the sauce thickens. Add cream cheese, Velveeta, and mozzarella; whisk until melted. (If the sauce gets too thick, then add a bit more milk and whisk.) Pour sauce over the macaroni, add salt, and combine. I always taste mine at this point, being careful not to burn my tongue, to make sure it has enough salt. Pour into a baking dish and top with Colby Jack. Bake for about 5 to 7 minutes, until cheese is golden and bubbly.

SPRING

Black-Eyed Peas with Snaps

Black-eyed peas are a totally Southern thing. We have mass amounts of them in the summer, and they go so well with a fried chicken dinner. The ones that don't go on the plate are frozen for the winter. We serve them on New Year's Eve because they bring prosperity to all who eat them—at least that's what my grandma said. My mama would always put a dried black-eyed pea in her pocketbook to make sure that she would have money the rest of the year. I don't know that it did any good, because I don't remember us having a whole lot of money growing up, but that's what had been passed down over the generations.

Make about 4 cups

3 cups water

2 cups fresh or frozen (thawed) black-eyed peas with snaps

1 hunk leftover ham, or 4 thick slices smoked ham, chopped

Salt and pepper

Place water in a saucepan and add the black-eyed peas and snaps. Add ham and bring to a boil. Turn heat down and simmer for about 1 hour, until black-eyed peas are tender. You may need to add a bit more water during the cooking process if the water cooks down too much. You want plenty of juice. Season with salt and pepper to taste.

Tomato, Cucumber, and Feta Salad

When I was a girl, we would occasionally go to the local cafeteria to eat lunch. The first time that I went, I was mesmerized. You pushed your tray down the line, and first came the salads—a smorgasbord of salads that even a kid could get excited over. If we knew ahead of time that we were going, my brothers and I would lay out a strategy of what we would eat, with the seriousness of plotting a battle in wartime. I always got the cucumber and tomato salad and have made my own version of it over the years, adding feta, as it is one of my favorite cheeses and I can get it freshly made from one of our neighbors, who raises goats.

Makes about 3 cups

1 cucumber, chopped

2 tomatoes, chopped

4 ounces feta cheese (or more if you like)

3 tablespoons chopped fresh basil

Salt and pepper

Place the cucumber, tomatoes, feta, and basil in a bowl. Season with salt and pepper to taste. Toss together and serve.

Peach Cobbler

You don't have to go to Georgia to find the best peaches; they can be had right here in Texas, and in summer you can find them as easily as you can swat a mosquito. Farm stands line the highways and every farmers market is loaded with vendors touting the best peaches.

This cobbler is made the way my grandmother made it. I do not like thick biscuit crust on my cobbler, so I use pie crust; I guess this could be more of a peach pie, but I make it in a square baking pan. Here's a great tip: Place your pan on a cookie sheet while baking. If it boils over, it is much easier to clean a cookie sheet than the bottom of the oven.

Makes 4 servings

5 cups sliced peaches

2/3 cup sugar

1/3 cup all-purpose flour

1/4 teaspoon cinnamon

2 Homemade Pie Crusts (page 93)

Preheat the oven to 400 degrees.

In a large bowl, combine the peaches, sugar, flour, and cinnamon. Fit one pie crust a into an 8 x 8-inch square baking dish. Fill crust with peach filling. Top with the other pie crust and crimp the edges to seal. Bake for about 30 minutes, until crust is golden brown.

LADIES DAY LUNCHEON

Cranberry Chicken Salad 66

Pimento Cheese-Stuffed Celery 69

Classic Cucumber Sandwiches 70

Lime Sherbet Punch 71

Coconut Cake 72

I love the small town feel of a ladies luncheon. Whether it is for garden club, art club, or just an excuse to throw a get-together, count me in. Our back patio always reminds me of a certain historic hotel where we've stayed in New Orleans. I had to have the aged brick floor and, of course, an old fountain because I love the sound of trickling water. Lush plants sway about, and it feels like a getaway even though it is just outside the back door.

What a great place to have a luncheon, I decided. I wanted to have a vintage-style luncheon complete with the lime sherbet punch that was always served for any occasion when I was growing up. You can throw it together with a moment's notice, and on a hot summer day, it is absolutely delicious. No self-respecting Southern woman would ever have a luncheon without pimento cheese or chicken salad, so of course, I have my own versions that have been passed down and perfected.

With the garden tables, my cherished faded pink swan, and a vintage paper umbrella, the décor is girly, dreamy, and all about the garden.

This would be a great menu for any little gathering of the girls, so start planning to serve up some of these Southern favorites.

Cranberry Chicken Salad

Everyone on earth has their own chicken salad recipe. It is a staple here in the South and has always been the go-to dish for all occasions. It's the perfect thing on a hot day when you don't want anything too heavy. For a special occasion, I make sandwiches and cut them into shapes. Make sure to use good-quality bread02. I've tried it with less-expensive bread and it just falls apart.

Makes about 6 cups

3 boneless, skinless chicken breasts, baked and chopped, or 1 rotisserie chicken, deboned and chopped (about 3 cups)

1/4 cup dried cranberries

3 sticks celery, finely chopped

1/4–1/2 cup pecans, finely chopped

2 tablespoons sweet pickle relish

1/2 cup mayonnaise

Mix together the chicken, cranberries, celery, pecans, and relish. Add mayonnaise and mix thoroughly. Chill until ready to serve.

SPRING

Pimento Cheese-Stuffed Celery

I remember that my other grandmother, my mama's mother, would always serve stuffed celery at Christmas. It would be sitting on the table, before all of the main dishes, alongside the deviled eggs and the olive tray. As kids, we would sneak in there and grab a stuffed celery, pushing the remaining ones together to hide the offense and grabbing a deviled egg on the way out. This is basically my favorite pimento cheese recipe stuffed into a celery stalk, but it looks rather fancy and tastes delightful. This is a great appetizer for a ladies luncheon or any lunch that you serve. The pimento cheese makes a great sandwich too.

1 cup grated Colby Jack cheese

1 cup grated sharp cheddar

8 ounces cream cheese, softened

1 (4~ounce) jar pimentos, drained

1/2 cup mayonnaise

Salt and pepper

12 sticks celery, cut into 4~inch strips

Place the cheeses, pimentos, and mayonnaise in a bowl. Season with salt and pepper to taste. Combine thoroughly.

Fill the celery with pimento cheese and watch them disappear.

Classic Cucumber Sandwiches

This is a traditional tea sandwich that has been served at many Southern social gatherings over the years. I like to make them for lunch, as they seem special and fancy, sort of a little treat for just a regular day. This was Aunt Kim's favorite sandwich. They go great with some good ol' salty potato chips or a salad, depending on who is showing up for lunch.

Makes about 4 1/2 cups

1 cucumber, peeled, seeded, and sliced

3 green onions, finely chopped

1 (8-ounce) package cream cheese, softened

1/4 cup mayonnaise

Salt and pepper

Sturdy white bread, thinly sliced

Place the cucumbers in a food processor to finely chop. Transfer to paper towels to drain. Pat cucumbers dry with paper towels and place in a bowl. Mix in the green onions, cream cheese, and mayonnaise. Season with salt and pepper, to taste. Spread cucumber mixture on slices of bread, leaving edges free of filling, as they will be cut off. Cut into desired shapes and serve chilled or at room temperature.

Lime Sherbet Punch

Back in the day, it was not a party without some sort of punch. Whether it was a wedding shower or a birthday party, we had punch. It made the event seem so much more special. This is an old standby recipe for any occasion. As I write this, I can see the ladies in their gloves and hats, standing around the punch bowl at a garden party luncheon. (You could hear the best gossip standing around the punch bowl!) There is nothing better than this refreshing punch that tastes like a ginger ale and lime float. I remember waiting at any a birthday party as my mama poured this punch into the themed paper cups that I had picked out for the occasion. Cheers to punch and parties—let's carry on the delicious tradition!

Makes about 8 cups

1 quart lime sherbet

1 liter ginger ale, chilled

Place lime sherbet in a punch bowl and pour the ginger ale over the top. Stir and let sherbet melt into the punch a bit before serving.

Coconut Cake

Everyone in our family loves coconut, so this cake disappears in a hurry. It is a light and fluffy cake that not only tastes good but is easy to make.

Makes 1 (9-inch) four-layer cake

1 box golden cake mix, prepared according to package directions for 2 round layers

16 ounces sour cream

2 cups sugar

14 ounces coconut, divided

4 ounces frozen whipped topping, thawed

Strawberries, for garnish, optional

Once the cakes have cooled, slice each one in half horizontally.

To make the filling, mix the sour cream, sugar, and 10 ounces of the coconut in a large bowl. Reserve 1/2 cup filling for the icing. Stack the first cake layer on a cake plate or serving dish. Spread one-third of the filling onto the cake, letting the filling spill over the sides. Repeat with two more cake layers. Top the cake with the final layer.

Mix the whipped topping with the reserved 1/2 cup filling. Ice the cake top and sides with this mixture. Sprinkle the remaining 4 ounces coconut onto the top and fill in any bare spots by pressing coconut onto the sides. Garnish the top with sliced strawberries, if desired. Refrigerate until serving.

Fourth of July Barbeque   81

Celebrate Charlotte   95

Fish Fry and Fish Favorites   119

Sandwiches   131

Summer

Summer is the best time of year, with a school's-out atmosphere and warm, starry nights just right for dining outdoors. The garden is at its peak, with juicy, red-ripe tomatoes ready to be picked from the vines. The crickets sing from across the lake as we sit on the porch with a glass of wine before dinner. Mid-summer means a Fourth of July barbeque, just like papa would have had at his country house. Luscious barbeque ribs, juicy brisket, along with all of the fixings—ideal for a picnic to remember.

Summer is perfect for creating what I like to call "food memories." Many of our reminiscences are filled with thoughts of holidays or gathering around the table for suppers with family and friends. You always remember what was served, how it smelled, and now it makes your mouth water just thinking about it. Not only that, but summer allows us to kick off our shoes, feel the earth between our toes, and hear the slam of the screen door. Those thoughts race across your brain as you think back on those special times. Life is all about moving forward and continuing to build memories that future generations will cherish. Letting the whole family see the food-growing process is important. It is great for them to be able to plant seeds, take care of the plants, and later eat the juicy tomatoes or squash that they planted. Children need to see how important cooking is and how these recipes are made and passed down.

In the summer, something as simple as a cane pole and a line can become a source for tonight's fish fry. Sitting out on the bank with the hum of locusts in the background you can watch a ring of water ripple from the bobber as a fish pulls the line. Just being outdoors, lazing on the shore and hearing the sound of nothing but nature is a true pleasure. When the heat gets a bit too warm, you slip off your shoes and dip your feet in the water or dangle them off of the dock. An impromptu fireworks show can happen anytime out here, and we love watching the giant explosions of color and their reflections dancing across the lake.

When the garden is coming in with a bountiful harvest, it is time for some delicious fare— from homemade lasagna with fresh basil or a garden casserole to Uncle Chad's Caprese Salad or perhaps a shrimp BLT for lunch. We relish having homegrown tomatoes at nearly every meal. These recipes will enhance your summer memories too, so let's get cooking.

FOURTH OF JULY BARBEQUE

Easy Barbeque Ribs   85

Aunty Lou's Brisket   86

Southern Mashed Potato Salad   87

Mexican Cole Slaw   88

Deviled Eggs   89

Sugar-Free Cherry Pie   90

I used to be intimidated to barbecue on my own. Joe was always the guy on the grill, but there are times when he is working late and I want to make some ribs, so I figured out how to make some delicious barbeque right in the oven. I think the pictures are a testimony to just how juicy and good those baby back ribs really are. And how about that cherry pie?

There is a spot by the barn under a tree where there is always a breeze, even in the July heat; it is a pretty spot to have a barbeque. Every year, I break out the decorations—and let me just tell you, I have decorations for any and all occasions, because I do love a party. I am all about vintage, so all of my flags and banners are old. I bought a giant flag at a flea market years ago and it serves us well every Fourth. The pole flag that stands on the edge of the barn is from an old elementary school in Nebraska. It was sold in a sale and then ended up down here in another Texas flea market, where I picked it up. There were actually two of them, but one year the kids decorated a float with the vintage flagpoles and as they passed under the trees, one of the flagpoles snapped, so now we have one. They won first prize on the float that year, so that was a good thing.

A small-town Fourth is the place to be, with chilled watermelon begging you to take a bite and let the juice drip down your chin; or watching the fireworks that come from all directions down this long gravel road. Out in the middle of nowhere can be a pretty great place to be. As we are stuffed to the brim with our Fourth of July food, we all sit back in our chairs or sprawl on a blanket across the grass, watching the kids run across the field with sparklers while fireworks dance across the sky.

Happy summer!

SUMMER

Easy Barbeque Ribs

You know, I always thought that ribs had to be cooked on the grill and that it was some big ordeal to be able to make good ribs. I was intimidated until a friend of mine told me that you can make them in the oven and they are absolutely delicious. After years of eating these, they are still one of Alex's favorite things and she always asks for "ribbies." This is an easy recipe and you can have mouthwatering ribs in just a few hours.

1–2 racks baby back ribs

Salt and pepper

1–2 bottles of your favorite barbeque sauce

Preheat oven to 300 degrees. Line a cookie sheet with a large piece of aluminum foil.

Take the ribs out of the plastic wrapper and wash them off. Then use a paper towel to dry them. Place the ribs on the foil-lined pan. Generously salt and pepper both sides of the ribs. Cover tightly with aluminum foil and place in oven. Let the ribs bake for 3 hours. Carefully remove ribs from the oven, open the foil, and spread the barbeque sauce generously over the top of the ribs. Leave ribs with the foil open and place back in the oven for 30 minutes, and then remove and serve.

Aunty Lou's Brisket

This is my Aunt Lou's brisket recipe. It is absolutely incredible and doesn't need a grill or smoker, which is great news for those that do not grill. I grew up down the street from Lou, and she and my mama have always been like sisters. She practically raised all of us kids in the neighborhood. She is like my second mom, so technically she is not my aunt, but she is to me. Aunt Lou can cook. Back when we were growing up, most moms cooked and shared recipes. The kids would run around all day, but in the evening you would hear the moms calling their kids for dinner. Sometimes we would get to eat at Aunt Lou's and you knew it was gonna be good. Here is Lou's recipe for brisket. She recommends not trimming the brisket before cooking, as the flavor is in the fat; trim it afterwards.

Rub:

4 tablespoons Liquid Smoke

2 teaspoons garlic powder

2 teaspoons onion salt

4 teaspoons celery salt

1 teaspoon salt

4 teaspoons Worcestershire sauce

4 teaspoons black pepper

10 pounds untrimmed brisket

Mix the rub ingredients in a bowl so that it looks like mud. Rub on the brisket, top and bottom, and then refrigerate. Let marinate for at least 2 hours. Preheat oven to 250 degrees and bake brisket for 6 to 7 hours.

Southern Mashed Potato Salad

Everyone has their favorite potato salad recipe and it's usually the one that you grew up with. My mama always made a mashed potato salad that I love. I know that some like it chunky and some like mayonnaise potato salad, but I grew up with mustard potato salad, and trust me, this one is good. Everyone in our family makes this same recipe. We served it along with the Mexican Cole Slaw at the Fourth of July barbeque this year and there was not a bite left.

Makes about 8~10 servings

6 large Russet potatoes

1/4 cup buttermilk

1 teaspoon salt

1 teaspoon pepper

2 hard~boiled eggs, 1 chopped and 1 sliced

2 sticks celery, diced

1 small purple onion, diced

2 medium kosher dill pickles, chopped

3 green onions, chopped, divided

2 1/2 heaping tablespoons yellow mustard

3 heaping tablespoons mayonnaise

4 strips crisp bacon, crumbled

Peel, dice, and boil the potatoes until tender. Drain potatoes and mash with the buttermilk, salt, and pepper. Add the chopped egg, celery, onion, pickles, half of the chopped green onions, mustard, and mayonnaise. Combine thoroughly and then add more salt and pepper to taste. Garnish with the sliced egg, crumbled bacon, and rest of the green onion.

Mexican Cole Slaw

This is one of those recipes that came from the newspaper years ago, back in the day when recipes were a big part of the newspaper because most everyone cooked. My mama could not wait to look through the grocery sale paper and peruse the recipes. I made this for the first time last year when the preacher was coming over for dinner. Now, you know when the preacher is coming for dinner, you've got to have something top notch, because you know that he goes to everybody's house and whether you know it or not, it is sort of a judgment. Well, I didn't want it getting around town that I just served the same old, same old, so after trying this cole slaw out prior to his visit, I knew that it would keep me in his good graces. We serve it for our Fourth of July barbeque and everybody loves it. It goes wonderfully with brisket or barbeque and is a delicious twist on traditional cole slaw.

Makes 6–8 servings

1 package cole slaw mix (I add some shredded cabbage to mine)

Shredded cabbage, optional

1 can black beans, drained

1 purple onion, chopped

1 can corn, drained

1 tomato, diced

4 tablespoons chopped cilantro

2 pickled jalapeños, diced

1 cup Ranch dressing

1 large avocado, sliced

Place all the ingredients, except avocado, in a bowl large enough to toss the salad, and mix well. Arrange slices of avocado on top of the salad.

Deviled Eggs

This is a recipe that everyone in the world needs to know. Everybody loves deviled eggs . . . well everybody that I know anyway. They are always the first thing to go, and we once had a near fight at the table as Uncle Charlie crammed the last deviled egg into his mouth. "Lordy, you just can't do that," my mama would say. I have seen him sneak off into the dining room before dinner and grab one or two off the plate. That poor old deviled egg plate was sitting there sporting two empty holes, and my mama would come in with the tea and see that and shake her head.

Everybody I know has a special dish for serving deviled eggs. This classic dish shows up at every potluck and funeral from here to the Louisiana line. If you don't know how to make deviled eggs then you better learn, because as my grandmother told me, "There is gonna come a time when you are gonna need to know how to make this," and she was right.

Makes 12

6 hard-boiled eggs

2 heaping tablespoons mayonnaise

2 heaping tablespoons mustard

1 tablespoon sweet pickle relish

2 strips crisp bacon, crumbled

Paprika, optional

Slice the eggs longways into halves. Remove yolk from eggs and place in a bowl. Add the mayonnaise, mustard, and relish and mix well. Scoop yolk mixture into the egg halves, filling the centers, and then top with crumbled bacon. If you like, you can add a light sprinkle of paprika over the tops of the eggs.

Sugar-Free Cherry Pie

Cherry Pie has always been a favorite for me. As a child, my mama's idea of homemade cherry pie was to open a can of cherry pie filling from the Busy Bee Grocery down the street. We all loved it. In fact, when I was only two years old, I might have loved cherry pie just a bit too much. My mother went into labor with my baby brother, and I was left at Mutty and Papa's house. Mutty was always cooking and had made cherry fried pies. I toddled around the kitchen and found the platter of cherry fried pies and proceeded to eat four of them before Mutty came back in to find me, but it was too late. They tell me that I was sick for two days. That incident did not darken my love of cherries. Who doesn't love the look of a bowl of cherries, they are so happy. It is hard to find good sugar-free recipes and this one is really good. When cherries are in season, you have to make a homemade cherry pie for yourself. You must remove the pits from all of the cherries, but after that . . . it is a cinch.

Makes one 9-inch pie

4 cups pitted cherries

1/2 cup water

1 cup Splenda or sugar

1 cup all-purpose flour

2 piecrusts (page 93)

Preheat oven to 400 degrees.

Place the cherries in large pot over medium heat. With a potato masher, squash cherries a bit to release juice, but still leaving them chunky. Add the water, Splenda, and flour. Mix the ingredients and let the filling simmer and thicken. Once it has thickened, remove from heat and let it cool. Pour into piecrust.

Top the cherry pie with strips of dough, interweaving every other row to make a lattice top. Then take a fork and crimp the edges. Bake until crust is golden and pie filling is bubbly, about 45 to 50 minutes. Cool thoroughly before eating.

SUMMER

Double-crust Piecrust

My grandmother always wore a gingham apron, and I can remember her rolling out pie dough on the counter. She made all kinds of pies and it did not have to be a special occasion. She used this same dough for her cobblers, too, but she always used a square or rectangle pan for those instead of a round pie pan. She would gather apples from a tree in the pasture and whip up a delicious apple pie and top it with vanilla ice cream. I loved her cherry pie and lemon meringue the best: her meringue stood taller than the beehive hairdo of my first grade teacher. On a holiday, my grandmother would always have at least three different flavors, and always pumpkin and pecan on Thanksgiving. This is a tried-and-true recipe that can be used for Chicken Pot Pie (page 154), fruit pie, or even a cobbler. Eat more pie!

Makes two 9-inch crusts

2 1/2 cups all-purpose flour

1/2 teaspoon salt

2 sticks butter, chilled and cut into 1/4-inch slices

1/3 cup ice water

Place flour and salt in a bowl and mix. Cut in the butter and mash with a fork until it becomes like course crumbs. Add ice water 1 tablespoon at a time until it reaches the right consistency. (I always add the ice water slowly, incorporating it well and making sure the dough is neither too sticky nor too dry. Divide dough into two balls then wrap in plastic wrap and refrigerate at least 1 hour.

Flour your work surface and roll out 1 ball of chilled dough into a large circle. Then set the pie pan upside down on top of dough and flip it over so the dough is in the pie pan; press dough lightly into the pan. Trim the edges and add filling. Then roll out the other ball of dough and slice into strips for the top of pie for lattice topping. For a regular top, just roll into a circle and place on top of pie. Trim edges and crimp them with a fork.

CELEBRATE CHARLOTTE

Sherry's Famous Beer Cheese Dip   98

Caesar Salad with Homemade Dressing   100

Carolyn's Best Lasagna   102

Pasta with Garden-Fresh Tomato Sauce   104

Uncle Chad's Tomato Caprese Salad   107

Chicken with Goat Cheese   110

Aunt Karen's Spaghetti   111

Parmesan Garlic Toast   112

Strawberry Champagne Punch   113

Grandmother's Fudge Cake   114

Strawberry Layer Cake   116

*W*e have many birthdays during the summer. Three fall in August—my husband Joe's, my mother Charlotte's, and mine. We decided that my mother's 80th birthday was a reason to Celebrate Charlotte. She has always been an inspiration. She was a well-known designer and artist and is still very active in the community. She has a great fashion sense, and she loves a good party as much as I. She told me not to play up the 80th part, so we focused on just the celebration and, of course, the food.

At first, this was supposed to be a dining al fresco party, under the trees on a summer night, which sounded magical. I would prepare most of the food with my homemade lasagna and pastas, while Chad and Sherri would bring a beautiful caprese salad and Beer Cheese Dip. I rented tables and tablecloths and we prepared for a lovely night under the stars. It turned out that the weather had different ideas. Two days before the party, we realized that is was probably going to rain. It hardly ever rains in August, but of course now it was going to rain. That changed everything. I sat on my bed late at night sketching out a new plan that would take place in our main hall, which luckily is forty feet long. I figured if we placed all of the tables end-to-end, then we could get everyone seated. I could string the lights over the tables by setting up vintage iron porch posts. I called the florist and added agapanthus to my order, which would look beautiful draping down with the lights. I had an old workbench that would make a perfect bar, and chalkboard wall panels made from thin wood and framed out would be great for chalk signage over the serving table and the bar. It was all coming together.

Like the overachiever, crazed mom and daughter that I am, I put together flower arrangements, strung lights and sheer fabric from the ceiling, and cooked food for the night. It was crazy, but it turned out magical. As my mama's friends entered the door, they gasped at the sight of the decor. That was all that I needed. As my mama was encircled at the door with her friends, smiling and laughing, it was all worth it.

This was the night of Charlotte and it was time to celebrate.

Sherry's Famous Beer Cheese Dip

This is a great dish for a Super Bowl party, tailgate, or any party where there are cheese lovers. It is wonderful served with pretzels, but I warn you that once you start, it is hard to stay away from this rich, creamy, delicious dip.

Makes about 3 cups

2 (8-ounce) packages cream cheese, softened

1 package Ranch dip mix

2/3 cup dark beer

1 cup shredded sharp cheddar cheese

1 cup shredded smoked Gouda cheese

Preheat oven to 350 degrees.

Mix all ingredients, except Gouda, together in an oven-safe pan, and bake for 25 minutes. Remove from oven and top the dish with smoked Gouda; put back into the oven and bake 5 more minutes, or until cheese is bubbly.

Caesar Salad with Homemade Dressing

This is my best friend Kim's easy and delicious version of Caesar salad. It is great served alongside lasagna, or on its own can be topped with grilled chicken.

6 cups torn Romaine lettuce

1/2 cup shaved or shredded Parmesan cheese

Salt

Cracked black pepper

Caesar Dressing, recipe below

Croutons (page 101)

Caesar Dressing:

2 tablespoons olive oil

2 cloves garlic

1 tablespoon Dijon mustard

Juice from 1 lemon, strained

2 dashes Worcestershire sauce

1/2 teaspoon cracked black pepper

Place lettuce in a salad bowl and sprinkle with Parmesan cheese, salt, and cracked pepper; toss. Add dressing and mix again. Serve topped with croutons.

For the dressing, mix all ingredients in a food processor and serve over salad.

Croutons:

1 tablespoon canola oil

1 stick (¹/₂ cup) butter

1 teaspoon garlic powder

¹/₂ loaf day~old French bread, cubed

Preheat oven to 350 degrees.

Melt the oil and butter in skillet on medium heat and stir in the garlic powder. Add bread cubes and mix them around in the garlic butter until well coated. Transfer bread cubes to a cookie sheet and place in the oven and bake until golden brown and crunchy.

Carolyn's Best Lasagna

I have made lasagna since before I met Joe, and it has always been a favorite for the whole family. When we decided to have a surprise birthday party for my mama, it was unanimous that we should serve lasagna. We ended up deciding to do an entire Italian dinner with the antipasto table and my Aunt Karen's spaghetti, which we adored as kids. The lasagna disappeared rather quickly. This was a wonderful night with the glowing lights and surrounded by friends, family, and our neighbors. As we bid everyone good-night, I think Nick and Joe were in the kitchen sneaking the last bits of lasagna from the pan.

Makes 12 servings

1 teaspoon salt and 1 tablespoon olive oil for pasta water

1 box of lasagna noodles

Sauce:

2 teaspoons olive oil

2 pounds ground beef

8 ounces breakfast sausage

1 large onion, diced

2 cloves garlic, minced

1 teaspoon garlic powder

1 tablespoon Italian seasoning

1 teaspoon dried basil

1/2 teaspoon salt

1/2 teaspoon pepper

1 jar prepared spaghetti sauce

1 (6-ounce) can tomato paste

1 (10-ounce) can diced tomatoes

Cheese:

2 cups ricotta cheese

1 egg

6 tablespoons milk

1/2 teaspoon salt

1/2 teaspoon pepper

2 cups shredded Colby Jack cheese

2 cups shredded mozzarella cheese

1/2 cup shredded Parmesan cheese

2 leaves fresh Basil, chopped, optional

Bring a large stockpot of water to a boil. Add 1 teaspoon salt and 1 tablespoon olive oil, then slide the lasagna noodles into the water. While boiling noodles until al dente, begin the sauce preparation. Once the noodles are done, drain and let them cool a bit so they can be handled for the lasagna construction.

Heat a large skillet over medium heat and add 2 teaspoons olive oil; then add the ground beef, sausage, and cook on medium heat, crumbling the meat as it cooks until almost done (still a little pinkish). Drain meat. Add the onion and garlic and sauté.

To the meat, add the garlic powder, Italian seasoning, basil, salt, and pepper. Cook meat until done and then add spaghetti sauce, tomato paste, and diced tomatoes. Stir and mix ingredients. Taste and adjust salt and pepper at this point. Simmer for 5 minutes.

Preheat oven to 375 degrees. In a bowl, mix together the ricotta cheese, egg, milk, salt, and pepper.

In a 9 x 12-inch baking pan, place a row of noodles covering the bottom. Spread with a small amount of meat mixture, covering noodles completely. Spread a layer of the ricotta mixture over meat mixture. Cover that layer with the Colby Jack, mozzarella, and Parmesan cheeses. Repeat this process, building layers and leaving enough cheese to cover the top of the casserole generously. Once assembled, place casserole in the oven and bake for 40 minutes, or until cheese is golden and bubbly. Garnish with fresh basil if you want.

Pasta with Garden-Fresh Tomato Sauce

This is probably one of the simplest recipes that you could ever make. It is best served when fresh tomatoes are in season.

Makes 6–8 servings

4 tablespoons olive oil

6 tablespoons butter

2 cloves garlic, minced

1 large onion, chopped

6 tomatoes, chopped

8 basil leaves, chopped

1 teaspoon salt

1/2 teaspoon cracked pepper

Penne pasta, linguini, or spaghetti, for serving

1/4 cup freshly grated Parmesan cheese

Heat olive oil, butter, garlic, and onion in a large skillet over medium heat and cook until onions are soft. Add fresh chopped tomatoes, basil, salt, and pepper. Serve over linguini or spaghetti and sprinkle with the Parmesan cheese.

SUMMER

Uncle Chad's Tomato Caprese Salad

Uncle Chad had thousands of these cherry tomatoes coming up all over his yard. Some were planted the year before and the birds scattered the seeds, so they came up everywhere. They made the most wonderful salad.

4 cups red~ripe cherry tomatoes (preferably home~grown)

1 (8~ounce) mozzarella/ prosciutto roll, cubed

1 (8~ounce) container mozzarella balls, drained

1/2 cup Greek Vinaigrette dressing

Salt and pepper

6 sprigs basil, chopped

Place tomatoes, cheese-prosciutto cubes, and mozzarella balls in a bowl. Pour on the dressing and sprinkle with a little salt and pepper; toss to coat well. Garnish with fresh basil.

Chicken with Goat Cheese

Alex and I had this one day at an Italian restaurant while in the city. She loved it, so I made my own version at home. It is one of her favorite dishes that I make. I serve it over pasta or rice.

Makes 4 servings

2 boneless, skinless chicken breasts

Salt and pepper

4 tablespoons olive oil, divided

2 cloves garlic, minced

1 fresh tomato, diced

1 medium onion, minced

1/4 cup chopped fresh basil (reserve 2 teaspoons for garnish)

1 1/2 teaspoons Italian seasoning

2 cups tomato pasta sauce (your favorite brand)

4 large slices goat cheese

1 cup shredded mozzarella cheese

Preheat oven to 350 degrees.

Wash and pat dry your chicken breasts and slice each breast in half lengthwise to make breasts thinner. You will have 4 halves. Season with salt and pepper.

Heat a skillet on low heat and add 2 tablespoons of olive oil. Add the garlic and sauté, stirring so the garlic does not burn. Once the garlic is soft, add tomato and onion and sauté until soft, stirring constantly. Add the basil and Italian seasoning along with the tomato pasta sauce. Turn heat up to medium and simmer the sauce for about 5 minutes. Remove sauce from pan. Rinse the skillet and then add and heat remaining 2 tablespoons olive oil.

Place chicken in a the skillet and sauté on medium heat for 8 minutes, turning chicken every so often so it does not scorch. In between turnings, cover chicken with a lid to keep the moisture in. After 8 minutes, remove chicken and place in an oiled baking dish to prevent sticking. Take the slices of goat cheese and place one on each chicken breast; then pour the sauce over the breasts. Sprinkle mozzarella cheese over each breast and place in oven to bake until cheese is hot and bubbly. Garnish the top with freshly chopped basil.

Aunt Karen's Spaghetti

This recipe was passed on to my mama from my Aunt Karen. As kids, we absolutely loved it and begged our mama to make it. I mean, come on . . . who wouldn't love a batch of cheesy spaghetti?

2 tablespoons olive oil

1 onion, chopped

2 cloves garlic

1 1/2 pounds ground beef, cooked and drained

1 tablespoon Italian Seasoning

1 (14.5~ounce) can tomato soup plus 3/4 can water

10 green olives, chopped

8~ounce log Velveeta, cubed

1 pound spaghetti or linguini, cooked al dente

3 basil leaves, chopped

To a skillet over medium heat, add olive oil, onion, and garlic. Sauté until onion is soft. Add cooked meat, Italian Seasoning, tomato soup, water, green olives, and Velveeta. Keep cooking and stir to incorporate all ingredients. When cheese has melted and sauce has had time to simmer, then remove from heat. If sauce is too thick, add a bit of water and mix until sauce is the right consistency and thoroughly heated. Serve over spaghetti noodles and garnish with freshly chopped Basil.

Parmesan Garlic Toast

This recipe is the way that we have always made our garlic bread. I have not seen any of my friends do it in quite the same way. It is really tasty.

1 stick (¹/2 cup) butter

1 tablespoon olive oil

1 teaspoon garlic powder

1 loaf French bread

¹/2 cup shredded Parmesan cheese

Preheat oven to 400 degrees.

Place butter and oil in a skillet on medium heat. Add the garlic powder. Slice the bread into thick slices. Place a piece of foil large enough to wrap around the French bread on a cookie sheet.

Dip bread slices into the garlic butter mixture and place on foil. Sprinkle with Parmesan cheese. Once all the pieces are in the foil, press foil closed and place in the oven. Bake for 10 minutes and then open foil and bake until golden.

Strawberry Champagne Punch

This punch is famous at our parties. It's really delicious, but it can pack a punch. We always serve it at our New Year's soiree. It goes great with holiday fare but is delectable any time of year.

Makes about 12 cups

2 pints whole fresh strawberries (reserve 8 strawberries for garnish)

²/₃ cup Grand Marnier

Crushed ice

2 fifths champagne, chilled

1 liter ginger ale, chilled

Wash strawberries and pat dry. Slice strawberries and place in a punch bowl. Add Grand Marnier and let soak for 30 minutes. Add crushed ice to bowl and pour champagne and ginger ale over the ice. Gently stir. Add a few strawberries as a garnish if desired.

Grandmother's Fudge Cake

This is one of our generational recipes, a sheet cake that we slice up and serve on a cake plate, like brownies. We always sprinkle toasted pecans over the fudgy icing. Our preacher says that he is on standby whenever we make this cake. I text him and I think he races to the house to get it—really! He eats two or three pieces and then wants a to-go box, which makes everybody else mad because my husband wants a piece every night. Pastor Kevin says that he is taking the cake home to his wife and daughter, but we know he is cramming cake in his mouth while driving down the road home. I think Joe is a sweet hog, and so is Pastor Kevin, for that matter. He might need to pray about overindulging . . . LOL.

Makes 12–15 servings

2 cups all-purpose flour

1 cup sugar

1 teaspoon baking soda

1/2 teaspoon baking powder

1/4 teaspoon salt

1 stick (1/2 cup) butter

1/3 cup canola oil

1 cup water

1/4 cup cocoa

2 eggs, slightly beaten

1/2 cup buttermilk

1 teaspoon vanilla extract

Chocolate Frosting (page 115)

Preheat oven to 350 degrees. Spray a 9 x 12-inch sheet cake pan with nonstick oil.

Sift the flour, sugar, baking soda, baking powder, and salt into a large mixing bowl. In a saucepan, melt the butter then add canola oil, water, and cocoa and simmer for 2 minutes. Pour the wet mixture over dry ingredients and stir to combine.

In a separate bowl, combine eggs and buttermilk then pour into the cake batter. Add the vanilla and stir. Pour batter into the cake pan and bake for about 35 to 40 minutes, until a toothpick inserted into the center of the cake comes out clean. Let cake cool to warm before frosting.

Chocolate Frosting:

1 stick (1/2 cup) butter

4 tablespoons cocoa

2 cups powdered sugar

1 teaspoon vanilla extract

1 tablespoon milk, as needed

1/4 cup chopped pecans, toasted

Melt the butter in a saucepan on medium heat; add the cocoa and stir to mix together. Remove from heat and stir in powdered sugar until smooth. Add vanilla, and add milk as needed if frosting is too thick.

Spread frosting on top of cake while it is warm (not hot) and sprinkle toasted pecans on top.

Strawberry Layer Cake

This is my favorite cake. With my birthday being in August, this was always my birthday cake. My son-in-law, Jose Luis, loves it too.

Makes 1 (9-inch) four-layer cake

1 package moist yellow cake mix

Cream Cheese Frosting:

8 ounces cream cheese

1/2 cup sugar

12 ounces non-dairy frozen whipped topping, thawed

1 cup powdered sugar

Strawberry Glaze:

3/4 cup sugar

3 tablespoons cornstarch

3/4 cup water

2 pints strawberries, chopped (reserve 5 whole berries)

Prepare two 9-inch round cake pans. Preheat oven and bake the cake according to package directions for a two-layer cake; cool completely. Slice the layers in half and place in the freezer.

Using an electric mixer, combine the cream cheese, sugar, whipped topping, and powdered sugar until well blended. Set aside.

For the glaze, in a saucepan combine the sugar and cornstarch; then stir in the water and strawberries. Bring to a boil and cook, stirring, for 3 to 4 minutes, until glaze thickens.

To assemble, place 1 frozen half of a cake layer on a cake plate. Spread a thin coat of the cream cheese mixture on the layer and then a thin layer of glaze. Repeat process with 2 more frozen halves and set the fourth layer on top. Cover the top of the cake with the remaining cream cheese mixture and spread remaining glaze over the icing.

Slice the 5 remaining whole strawberries and garnish the top of the cake. Refrigerate until time to serve.

FISH FRY AND FISH FAVORITES

Hush Puppies   120

Cole Slaw   121

Fried Catfish   122

Almond~Crusted Salmon   124

Southern Salmon Patties   126

Dad's Fish Dipping Sauce   127

Green Tomato Relish   128

Spicy Garlic Pickles   129

Hush Puppies

There isn't a fish fry in the South that doesn't have hush puppies. Our volunteer fire department puts on the fish fry every year, and yes there are always hush puppies. Just like everything else, there is nothing like homemade. When I am whipping up some fried catfish that Nick has caught at the lake, I always make up some hush puppies to go with it. You know, I would say they are as good as the fish . . . yum.

1 cup yellow cornmeal

1/4 cup all-purpose flour

1 1/2 teaspoons baking powder

1/2 teaspoon salt

1 egg, beaten

3/4 cup buttermilk

1 small onion, finely chopped

3 pickled jalapeños, finely chopped, optional

Oil for frying

In a bowl, mix the cornmeal, flour, baking powder, and salt together. Add the egg and buttermilk and whisk. Add the onion and jalapeños if desired, and stir to combine.

Pour oil in a cast iron skillet to a depth of at least halfway up the side. Heat on medium-high to 350–375 degrees. When you drop in a bit of batter, the oil should sizzle. Drop spoonfuls of round hush puppy batter into the oil and fry until golden brown. Drain on paper towels before serving.

Cole Slaw

You are going to love this cole slaw. It has just the right balance of sweet and tart taste and is not too heavy. What I think makes the difference in cole slaw is the freshness of the cabbage. The slaw mix that is pre-shredded is white and also dry. I know it is an extra step, but it makes all the difference in the world to shred your own cabbage and carrots. You will taste the difference.

1/2 cup mayonnaise

2 tablespoons white vinegar

2 tablespoons sugar

1/2 teaspoon cracked black pepper

1/2 teaspoon celery salt

Salt

1 head green cabbage, shredded

2 carrots, peeled and shredded

2 green onions, finely chopped

In a bowl, whisk together the mayonnaise, vinegar, sugar, pepper, celery salt, and salt to taste.

Place the cabbage, carrots, and green onions in a bowl. Pour the dressing over the vegetables toss to thoroughly coat.

Fried Catfish

Across the tiny gravel road from our place there is a large tank on our property that stretches about two acres. It's called "the lake." When my children were small we would go on nature walks and always ended up there, to watch the snapping turtles as they sunned on the old fallen tree. In over 150 years the lake has never gone dry, so it must be very deep. As my son, Nicholas, grew older, he spent most of his time at the lake, fishing and watching the ducks. He and his friends are still fishing there, and they have brought me some wonderful sand bass to fry up over the years, along with catfish. Nick cleans them and I do the frying. Mutty used to fry our fish that we caught from their tank, and she always used Quaker cornmeal, so that is what I use. Nothing is better than a crispy piece of fish; whether from the seafood market or from the tank across the road, it is all good. Y'all enjoy.

Makes 8 servings

**8 fish fillets,
cleaned and deboned**

2 cups buttermilk

2 cups canola oil

2 cups cornmeal

1 teaspoon salt

1 teaspoon lemon pepper

**1 teaspoon granulated
garlic**

**Tartar Sauce, recipe
below**

Soak fish in buttermilk and while waiting, heat the oil in cast iron skillet until bubbling, 350 degrees. Mix the cornmeal, salt, lemon pepper, and garlic together in a wide pan or bowl suited for dredging. Coat the fish on both sides with cornmeal and place into hot oil; fry for about 4 minutes, turning, until it is golden brown. Remove from skillet and place on paper towels. Enjoy with tartar sauce.

Tartar Sauce:

1 cup mayonnaise

**2 tablespoons dill pickle
relish**

**A couple of dashes
Tabasco sauce, optional**

Almond-Crusted Salmon with Spring Greens and Blue Cheese

I have had salmon many times at restaurants, and very few times have I thought that it had much flavor. This salmon is full of flavor. My kids do not order salmon out at a restaurant anymore because they like mine, which is quite a compliment. The fish sort of blackens in the teriyaki sauce, and the crunch of the almonds, the crispness of the greens, the saltiness of the blue cheese . . . well, it makes my mouth water.

Makes 2 servings

2 salmon fillets, skin removed

Salt and pepper

1 cup coarsely crushed almonds

3 tablespoons olive oil

1 clove garlic, minced

Juice from 1 lemon

2 tablespoons teriyaki sauce

2 cups field greens

4 tablespoons blue cheese

2 tablespoons good balsamic vinegar

Rinse the fish fillets in water and pat dry with a paper towel. Salt and pepper the fillets then dredge in coarsely crushed almonds until well coated.

In medium skillet, heat the olive oil on medium-low then add the garlic and stir. Jut before adding fish to the pan, increase heat to medium, making sure not to burn the garlic. Lay the fillets in the oil and squeeze lemon over the fish. Pour the teriyaki sauce over the fillets. Sauté until fish is flaky and firm.

Arrange the field greens on two plates. Move the almond crusted salmon fillets from the pan and set on the beds of field greens. Sprinkle with blue cheese and drizzle with balsamic vinegar.

Southern Salmon Patties

This southern recipe is great, even for people that don't like salmon. Most everybody loves a good fried salmon patty, or croquette, as we good southern folks like to call them. I always serve my daddy's fish sauce with these patties, along with mashed potatoes and spinach. Nicholas can eat almost a whole platter by himself, and he is standing there right by the skillet as they come out of the pan. Scrumptious!

Makes 6–8 servings

2 (14.75-ounce) cans pink salmon, drained

1 large onion, finely chopped

2 tablespoons mayonnaise

2 tablespoons mustard

1/2 teaspoon lemon pepper

2 eggs, whisked

1 1/2 cups cornmeal, divided

1/2 teaspoon salt

1/2 teaspoon pepper

1 cup canola oil

1 cup cornmeal

Dad's Fish Dipping Sauce (page 127)

Place the salmon in a large bowl and remove any bones and skin.

Mix the salmon together with the onion, mayonnaise, mustard, lemon pepper, eggs, 1/2 cup cornmeal, salt and pepper. Form into patties.

Heat the oil to about 350–375 degrees in a cast iron skillet on medium heat. Dredge the patties in remaining 1 cup cornmeal. Test the oil by dropping in a bit of cornmeal; when it sizzles, the oil is hot enough. Add patties to the skillet and fry until golden brown and then turn gently. Once the other side is golden, remove patties and place on paper towels to drain. Serve with Dad's Fish Dipping Sauce.

Dad's Fish Dipping Sauce

This is another one of my daddy's concoctions. We have made this sauce my entire life and growing up this is what we used on our fish and our fried shrimp.

Makes about $1/2$ cup

2 tablespoons mustard

2 tablespoons ketchup

2 tablespoons mayonnaise

1 teaspoon sweet relish

2 dashes Tabasco sauce

Mix all the ingredients together thoroughly. Refrigerate any leftover sauce.

Green Tomato Relish

Sometimes I think that I like the green tomato relish more than the catfish. This goes great with any fish recipe.

8 large green tomatoes, chopped

2 cups finely chopped onion

3 cups sugar

1 cup seeded and chopped jalapeños (make sure to remove the veins)

2 cups white vinegar

1/2 cup salt

Place tomatoes, onions, sugar, jalapeños, vinegar, and salt into a large cooking pot. Mix well and simmer over medium heat, stirring, until tomatoes turn from green to brownish and steam begins to form. Be sure not to overcook or let the mixture boil. They are ready for canning. Follow current safe canning procedures to bottle the tomato relish.

Spicy Garlic Pickles

Who doesn't love a crispy, garlicky, spicy pickle? Our family can go through a jar a day. This is the recipe that Mutty used. When the cucumbers start bearing well or if you can stop by the farmers market and pick some up, this is a great recipe to try.

Makes 8–10 pints

36 medium pickling cucumbers, washed, dried, and sliced

4 cups water

2 cups apple cider vinegar

2 cups white vinegar

1/2 cup pickling salt

Spice bag: in cheesecloth add 2 tablespoons black peppercorns, 2 tablespoons mustard seed, and 2 tablespoons dill seed; knot the cheesecloth

16–20 cloves garlic, cleaned and slightly smashed (2 per jar)

30 black peppercorns (3 per jar)

10 sprigs fresh dill (2 per jar)

8–10 fresh cayenne peppers (1 per jar)

1 1/2 teaspoons alum

Wash, dry, and slice the cucumbers; set aside. In a large pot, bring to a boil the water, vinegars, salt, and spice bag. Boil for 4 minutes.

Sterilize 8–10 quart jars as directed by current canning protocol. Once the jars are sterilized, fill with sliced cucumbers. Then add to each jar 2 cloves garlic, 3 peppercorns, 1 sprig dill, 1 cayenne pepper, and 1/8 teaspoon alum. Pour the brine solution carefully over the cucumbers in the jars, leaving 1/2 inch headspace. Seal and process in a canning bath according to current recommended canning instructions. Let the jars of pickles cool before shelving, and let stand for two weeks before enjoying.

SANDWICHES

Simply Perfect Shrimp BLT   132

Fried Baloney and Egg Sandwich   135

Simply Perfect Shrimp BLT

As if a regular BLT isn't good enough, this recipe adds just a few gorgeous grilled shrimp to make it even better. This is best in the summer when the tomatoes are homegrown—a couple of slabs of a big, red, juicy tomato really make it. I usually season the tomato with sea salt or a good pink salt. Oh, and you have to use good bread. This is best eaten outside while dining al fresco.

Makes 1 sandwich

2 strips thick-sliced bacon

4 jumbo shrimp, peeled, deveined, and tails removed

1 teaspoon lemon juice

2 slices good-quality bakery bread

3 tablespoons butter

1 tablespoon olive oil

1 teaspoon garlic powder

1/2 teaspoon chopped parsley

1 large leaf butter lettuce

2 thick slices homegrown tomato

Salt and pepper

Fry the bacon in a skillet over medium heat. Place the bacon on paper towels to drain. Sauté the shrimp in the bacon drippings until pink. (Be careful not to cook them too long or they will become rubbery.) Place on a paper towel to drain. Sprinkle the lemon juice over the shrimp.

Heat bread in a toaster until well toasted. Melt the butter and olive oil in a skillet. Add the garlic powder and parsley, stirring to mix. Swipe the toast through the butter and garlic mixture, covering one side of each piece of toast. Place one slice of toast on a plate buttery side up and layer the lettuce and tomato slices. Season the tomato with salt and pepper to taste, and then add the bacon and shrimp. Top with the other piece of toast and cut diagonally.

SUMMER

Fried Baloney and Egg Sandwich

Growing up, fast food was something that we very rarely ate because people cooked. Sometimes my daddy would get in the kitchen and whip up one of his favorites, and this is one of them. His dad, Papa, loved him some baloney. Daddy did too. He knew the butcher at this little corner store, and he would have them slice the baloney an inch thick, and you always had to have red-rind cheese—or rat cheese, as they called it. He was famous in our family for his fried baloney sandwich, but it had to be German baloney; he didn't like all-beef baloney for this sandwich. It's even better with a fried egg on top. My mouth is watering just thinking about it.

Makes 1 sandwich

2 slices good-quality bread

2 tablespoons canola oil

1 thick slice baloney

1 tablespoon mayonnaise

1 leaf fresh garden lettuce

2 slices homegrown tomato

1 slice purple onion

Salt and pepper

1 egg, fried hard

1 slice red-rind or Colby cheese

Preheat the broiler.

Toast the bread in a toaster. Meanwhile, pour the oil in a skillet and fry baloney over medium heat. Remove baloney and place on a paper towel.

Spread the toasted bread with mayonnaise. On one slice of toast, stack the lettuce, tomato, and then onion. Season with salt and pepper to taste. Place baloney on the other piece of toast, followed by the egg and the cheese. Put the cheese-topped slices on a baking sheet and place under the broiler to melt the cheese. When melted, combine the two slices of toast and cut sandwich in half.

Soup for Supper   141

Autumn Dinner Al Fresco   153

Halloween Barn Party   157

Meatloaf Monday   171

Autumn

When the first cool breeze blows in we are all on board for autumn. After a long, hot Texas summer, the chill in the air is welcome. As the leaves slowly start to turn colors and fall from the trees, I am thinking about building the first fire and cooking up a big pot of soup. Everyone knows my love of soup and I have many favorites. Not only do the recipes change for autumn, but so does my décor both inside and out. Pumpkins are harvested from the fields and piled on wagons; hay bales are trailing down porch stairs. Velvet pillows and lush, warm blankets are thrown about the house across tables, chairs and sofas. It is a time for softness, warmth and decadence. It is the season of comfort.

Almost like watching a progressive slide show, the environment changes from the hottest of hot to the first cool spell and then the first frost. I am, of course, known for my passion for decorating, so I am pulling out the orange plaid pillows that will deck out the porch chairs and rockers. Out with the summer décor and in with sunflowers, fall leaves, and, yes, vintage black bird cages, filled with crows. The barn is overhauled for the annual Halloween party, which has been going on for decades. The trees go from dark green to tans and oranges. The waning

zinnias are replaced with colorful pansies, and the menus change from garden fare and salads to hearty soups, rich dips, and delicious chili. Harvested hay bales sit among the fields, offering food to all of the farm animals.

It is the change of the season—it is autumn now.

SOUP FOR SUPPER

Down~Home Chicken and Dumplings 144

Broccoli and Cheese Soup 147

Nick's Cheeseburger in a Bowl Soup 148

Blue Ribbon Beef Stew 150

I can eat soup any time of year, but when that first cool breeze blows, the whole family is craving the warmth of soup. I am always about decorating and cooking for the seasons, so a dinner can take place literally anywhere. For autumn, a table is brought into the library so that we can enjoy dinners sitting in our fabulous leather club chairs that are torn and worn in just the right spots. And I love plopping down in one while enjoying a drink before supper. As the wind rustles the leaves on the trees just outside the library window, a fire crackles in the fireplace. Joe has a great love for my beef stew, and it is hearty with big chunks of beef amongst a gravy-like broth. And we also love chicken and dumplings. You will notice that most of my soups start with olive oil and garlic. I think I put fresh garlic in almost every soup that I make. It is good for you and adds so much to the flavor that I just cannot resist adding some. I usually start the soup in the same pot that it will cook in, so that none of the flavor is lost.

Tonight is a good night to snuggle up to a good bowl of homemade soup.

AUTUMN

Down-Home Chicken and Dumplings

Chicken and dumplings is just one of those dishes that make people feel better. It is total comfort food and it doesn't get any more Southern. My grandmother always used her biscuit recipe to make dumplings. You can do the same. Instead of cutting the biscuit dough into circles, cut dumplings into 1/2-inch strips. You are going to love this bowl of goodness.

Makes about 8–10 servings

1 recipe biscuit dough (see page 20), cut into 1/2-inch-wide strips

2 tablespoons canola oil

1 carrot, peeled and chopped

1 rib celery, strings pulled, finely chopped

1 whole chicken

4 cups water

2 cups chicken broth from cooking chicken

2 chicken bouillon cubes

1/2 teaspoon poultry seasoning

1 can evaporated milk

2 cups whole milk

Salt and pepper

Make the biscuit dough. Let rest while you cook the chicken.

Heat the oil in a sauté pan and cook the carrot and celery on medium heat until softened.

Place the whole chicken in a stockpot with the water and heat on high until it comes to a boil. Add carrots and celery. Bring back to a boil and continue cooking on medium high until chicken is fully cooked. Remove chicken and shred the meat.

Reheat 2 cups chicken broth on medium-high heat. Add the chicken bouillon cubes, poultry seasoning, evaporated milk, and whole milk. Add shredded chicken. Once the soup is boiling, turn heat down to medium and drop spoonfuls of biscuit dough into the boiling pot. Stir carefully to make sure dumplings stay intact. Once all dumplings are added, bring chicken to a boil and continue cooking until biscuits are cooked through, 5 minutes or more. Season to taste with salt and pepper.

AUTUMN

Broccoli and Cheese Soup

This is the ultimate comfort food in a bowl. It is thick, rich, and luscious. Making this soup takes only about 30 minutes, but you need to stir frequently. Go ahead—whip up a bowl and enjoy it while watching the sunset. In autumn the weather is still warm in Texas, and we find that by getting creative with an informal "table," we can enjoy our surroundings and have good conversation while we dine, not at all like it might be if we were mindlessly eating in front of the television.

2 tablespoons canola oil

6 tablespoons (3/4 stick) butter

1 onion, finely diced

2 ribs celery, finely diced

2 carrots, peeled and finely diced

1 clove garlic, minced

1 1/2 cups chopped broccoli

1/4 cup all-purpose flour

1 can evaporated milk

4 cups (32 ounces) chicken stock

2 cups milk

8 ounces Velveeta, cubed

Put oil and butter in a stockpot and melt on medium heat. Add onions, celery, carrot, garlic, and broccoli. Cook and stir until vegetables are slightly softened, about 7 to 10 minutes. Sprinkle the flour over vegetables and cook flour for 1 minute while stirring. Add the evaporated milk, stirring constantly while sauce thickens. Add the chicken stock and milk and bring to a simmer, stirring; cook for 10 minutes, stirring frequently. Add the cheese and stir constantly until cheese is melted and soup is thick and bubbly.

Nick's Cheeseburger in a Bowl Soup

This soup is great for a football game or tailgate party. Nick loves it any time. It sounds kind of crazy that it has the same ingredients as a cheeseburger, including the lettuce and tomato, but it works beautifully. Thick, rich, and filling, it has the familiar flavor of a favorite comfort food.

Makes 6–8 servings

2 tablespoons olive oil

1 large onion, diced

2 cloves garlic, minced

1 1/2 pounds ground beef, browned and drained

4 cups beef broth

1 tablespoon dill pickle relish

1 tablespoon prepared yellow mustard

1 large tomato, diced

1 teaspoon Worcestershire sauce

8 ounces Velveeta, cubed

1/2 teaspoon black pepper

1 cup shredded iceberg lettuce

Hamburger bun croutons

Real bacon bits, for garnish, optional

Shredded cheddar cheese, for garnish, optional

Heat olive oil in soup pot on medium heat and add onion and garlic. Stir until onion is softened. Add ground beef and beef broth and bring to a simmer. Add dill pickle relish, mustard, tomato, and Worcestershire sauce and simmer for 5 more minutes. Add cheese and let melt thoroughly. Simmer all ingredients for 10 to 12 minutes, stirring frequently. Add pepper and lettuce; remove from heat, still stirring. Lettuce will wilt into the soup. Garnish bowls of soup with hamburger bun croutons, real bacon bits, and shredded cheddar cheese, if desired.

Hamburger bun croutons:

1 hamburger bun

2 1/2 tablespoons (1/3 stick) butter

1 teaspoon garlic powder

Preheat oven to 350 degrees.

Take a hamburger bun (top and bottom) and dice it. Melt the butter in a skillet with the garlic powder. Drop bread cubes into butter and stir, coating cubes thoroughly. Place in an ovenproof pan and bake until crispy and golden.

Blue Ribbon Beef Stew

This is Joe's favorite thing in the world, even in the summer. This is my grandmother's recipe and my mama made it for us kids. I remember coming home from school one winter evening when a fire was roaring in the fireplace and my mom had the table set with red enamelware; a big pot of beef stew made the whole house smell wonderful. If you are craving warmth and comfort, this recipe will hit the spot.

Makes 6–8 servings

2 tablespoons olive oil

1–2 onions, chopped

2 cloves garlic, minced

6 carrots, diced

2 ribs celery, diced

1 cup all-purpose flour

2 pounds cubed stew meat

4 cups beef broth

1 teaspoon Worcestershire sauce

2 large potatoes, diced

1 bay leaf

1 teaspoon salt, plus more

1 teaspoon pepper, plus more

In large stockpot, heat the olive oil on medium heat. Add the onion, garlic, carrots, and celery and sauté until onion has softened.

Place flour in a bowl and dredge the stew meat. Add 1/2 cup of beef broth to the onion and carrot mixture in stockpot. Add meat and stir for a minute. Then add remaining beef broth, Worcestershire sauce, potatoes, bay leaf, salt, and pepper. Turn heat to low and simmer for 1 hour, until meat is tender. Remove bay leaf. Season to taste with salt and pepper.

AUTUMN

151

AUTUMN DINNER AL FRESCO

Chicken Pot Pie   154

Most people think of dining al fresco in the summertime, but in Texas and other Southern states it can be blazing hot until mid~October. So we love to celebrate the first cool breezes of fall. Our autumn celebrations come alive with rich fall plaid table runners and an urn spilling forth limbs gathered from the crepe myrtles and sunflowers picked from the fields. Pumpkins gathered from the patch are a colorful table detail.

This is how easy a gathering can be put together: take the kitchen table out into the yard and place the outdoor chairs around it. What a grand change of scenery! This is a perfect occasion to serve individual chicken pot pies in cast iron skillets.

In short order, the family is enjoying a celebration as easy as dining al fresco on a fall night.

Chicken Pot Pie

When I was growing up, my mama would buy the individual chicken pot pies in the frozen section of the grocery store, and we loved them. That was before I made a homemade chicken pot pie for the first time. There is no comparison, and a homemade pot pie is easy enough to make. You can make one big pot pie in a 9-inch pie pan or individual pot pies in smaller pans or ovenproof ceramic bowls. Either way, this is a delicious one-dish meal.

Makes 4 servings

2 tablespoons olive oil

1 white onion, diced

2 cloves garlic, minced

3 large boneless, skinless chicken breasts, diced

2 carrots, peeled and diced

2 ribs celery, diced

1 (12-ounce) package frozen corn, peas, and carrots, thawed

1 teaspoon salt

1/2 teaspoon pepper

1/2 cup all-purpose flour

1 cup whole milk

2 piecrusts (page 93)

Preheat oven to 350 degrees. Ready a 9-inch pie pan or 4 smaller ones.

Place olive oil in a medium saucepan and heat on medium heat. Add onion, garlic, and diced chicken and sauté for 5 minutes. Add carrots and celery and sauté for 5 more minutes. Add frozen vegetable and sauté until vegetables are warm. Add salt and pepper to taste. Sprinkle flour over mixture, add the milk, and whisk until thickened to a gravy consistency.

Prepare the pie pan (or smaller pans) by placing a piecrust in the bottom of the pie pan; then add filling on the top of the crust. Cover with the top pie crust and press edges together with a fork to seal. Vent the top with slits and place in oven and bake until crust is golden brown, about 35 to 40 minutes.

HALLOWEEN BARN PARTY

Venison Chili   160

Cheesy Spinach and Orange Pepper Dip   163

White Chili with Chicken   164

Nana's Bean Salad   165

Chocolate-Dipped Apples   168

Gummy Worm Pudding Cups   169

The pumpkin vines wind through the field with pumpkins of every shape and color: bright orange, dark green, and light green—and gourds are mixing about. The annual Halloween Barn Party has been going on for decades because we have birthdays around that time. Hay bales are sprinkled about the house and the barn, and are scattered with pumpkins. Pumpkins trail down porch stairs, spill from pots, and fill wagons. The barn gets a complete overhaul for this event. Lights are strung from the rafters and long tables line the center of the barn for everyone to have a place to sit and eat.

Everyone wriggles into the perfect spot to roast weenies over the fire, while all kinds of dishes are ready on the serving table: Nana's Bean Salad, a pretty spectacular Venison Chili, and a white chicken chili for those who aren't as gamey. Either one goes great with a hot dog. My Cheesy Spinach and Orange Pepper Dip is a pretty spectacular crowd pleaser too.

For a sweet treat, kids love the Gummy Worm Pudding Cups and the adults munch down on Chocolate-Dipped Apples. As the night wears on, toasted marshmallows are melted over chocolate bars and graham crackers for mouthwatering s'mores. Listen—what is that sound off in the distance? Is it a wolf—or just a dog howling down the country road? The ghost stories begin as I put another marshmallow over the flame, which has now died down to a perfect orange glow. I look up at the full moon and see wide eyes all around the fire as the spook tales come to a close.

The Halloween Barn Party is a success.

Venison Chili

This recipe has won the chili contest at our local chili supper, and it makes a big pot. When I make it, I use half venison sausage and half ground beef. I have also used wild hog sausage in place of the venison, and sometimes all ground beef. It's delicious made any way and is the hit of the weenie roast and Halloween party, when there's a bit of a chill in the air. This is superb used in a Frito pie or for chili dogs or with cornbread. Yum!

Makes enough for a crowd

2 tablespoons canola oil

4 pounds ground meat (2 pounds wild hog sausage or venison sausage mixed with 2 pounds ground beef, or all ground beef; you decide)

2 onions, chopped

3 cloves garlic, minced

1/2 cup chili powder

4 tablespoons cumin

2 teaspoons garlic powder

1/2–1 teaspoon salt

1 teaspoon cayenne pepper

1 1/2 teaspoons black pepper

3 1/4 cups water

1 (6-ounce) can tomato paste

1 (28-ounce) can crushed tomatoes

1 tablespoon masa

1 cup hot water

Chopped onion for garnish

Shredded cheese, for garnish

In a large stockpot, heat the oil over medium-high heat and add the meat; cook and stir until brown. Once the meat is browned, drain off the fat. Add onions and garlic to the meat and continue cooking until the onions soften. Add the chili powder, cumin, garlic powder, salt, cayenne pepper, and black pepper and mix well. Then add the water, tomato paste, and crushed tomatoes and mix in well. Let the chili simmer for 30 minutes on low heat, stirring occasionally.

Mix the masa in a small bowl with the hot water and add to the chili. Simmer for another 20 minutes, until thickened. Serve with a garnish of chopped onion and shredded cheese on top.

Cheesy Spinach and Orange Pepper Dip

One of the best parts about a party is that there are usually dips and desserts. I happen to love dip more than dessert. I developed this concoction when we had an overabundance of bell peppers coming from the garden. It's yummy!

2 tablespoons olive oil

1/2 cup chopped onion

2 orange bell peppers, finely chopped

2 cloves garlic, minced

2 cups chopped fresh spinach

1/2 teaspoon salt

1/4 teaspoon pepper

8 ounces cream cheese, softened

1 cup plain yogurt

1 cup shredded Colby Jack cheese, divided

1 cup shredded mozzarella cheese, divided

4 strips crispy bacon, crumbled

3 green onions, chopped, for garnish

Preheat oven to 350 degrees. Prepare a medium baking dish with nonstick spray.

Heat the oil in a medium saucepan over medium heat. Then add the onion, bell peppers, and garlic. Sauté until onions are soft. Add the spinach and cook until wilted, then add salt and pepper. Remove from heat.

In a separate bowl, mix together the cream cheese, yogurt, 1/2 cup Colby Jack, 1/2 cup mozzarella, and the spinach mixture until combined.

Pour mixture into the baking dish and spread evenly. Top with remaining cheese and crumbled bacon. Bake about 15 minutes, or until golden and bubbly. Remove from oven and garnish with green onions before serving.

White Chili with Chicken

Here in the South, chili is a staple. We have the chili cook-off every year, and this white chicken chili is an awesome variation of typical chili. It is rich and hearty, and people are amazed at how good it is, especially those who prefer chicken over beef. You have to try this one–you will be glad you did.

1 tablespoon vegetable oil

1 1/2 pounds boneless, skinless chicken breasts, cubed

1/2 cup all-purpose flour

1 onion, finely chopped

2 cloves garlic, minced

2 (14.5-ounce) cans chicken broth

2 (15.8-ounce) cans great Northern beans, drained and rinsed

1 (15.8-ounce) can pinto beans, drained and rinsed

2 (4.5-ounce) cans chopped green chiles, with liquid

1 1/2 teaspoons garlic powder

1 teaspoon ground cumin

1 teaspoon salt

1/2 teaspoon dried oregano

1 cup sour cream

1 cup whipping cream

2 cups shredded Monterey Jack cheese, divided

Cilantro, for garnish

In a large stockpot, heat the oil over medium heat.

Dredge the chicken in flour and begin cooking chicken. After 5 minutes, add the onion and garlic. Cook chicken and onion mixture for an additional 5 to 7 minutes, or until chicken is done.

Add the broth, beans, green chiles, garlic powder, cumin, salt, and oregano. Simmer for 30 minutes on low heat. Remove mixture from heat and whisk in the sour cream and whipping cream until incorporated. Then add 1 cup of cheese and mix together well until cheese is melted.

Serve and garnish with cilantro and remaining 1 cup cheese.

Nana's Bean Salad

Victoria's birthday is right around Halloween, so she always wanted a Halloween party. Her parties became famous and we ended up having 75 people over. Nana's Bean Salad has been a fixture at these parties. It is really easy and really tasty, especially with hot dogs and campfire fare. It is also great at a summertime barbeque.

Makes 6–8 servings

**1 (28-ounce) can pork
and beans**

1 yellow onion, chopped

**3 medium dill pickles,
chopped**

**1 tablespoon prepared
mustard**

**2 tablespoons
mayonnaise**

2 tomatoes, chopped

Mix all ingredients together in a medium-sized bowl and serve.

Chocolate-Dipped Apples

We make these every Halloween, when apples are abundant. It works best using small-to-medium red delicious apples, so that they fit well into the chocolate dip. The kids and I always made a fun project of going out to the woods to find the perfect size sticks to use as the handle for the apples while dipping. It adds a little something to use crooked sticks rather than the generic craft sticks. We generally use these as decoration, but they taste good at the end of the night or the following day. Parents need to do the dipping, as the chocolate can be a bit hot. If you plan to eat them, then do so immediately after they have cooled. But first remove the sticks and slice the apples.

Makes 4 apples

1–2 cups (14–16 ounces) prepared dipping chocolate for fruit

4 small red delicious apples, washed and dried

4 found sticks

1/2 cup crushed pecans

Heat the chocolate dip as directed on the package. Remove stems from the apples. Push sticks into the center of the apples where the stems were. Dip apples into the warm chocolate by holding the sticks. When coated, sprinkle apples with crushed pecans.

Gummy Worm Pudding Cups

Kids love to make these fun treats, and they are super easy. They also make great décor for a Halloween party. You can get really creative by surrounding them with candy corn and eyeball candy or whatever enhances your creepy décor.

2 (5.9-ounce) packages instant chocolate pudding mix

4 cups milk

1 cup frozen non-dairy whipped topping, thawed

1 cup crushed chocolate cookies with cream filling

Gummy worms, for garnish

Mix the chocolate pudding into the milk following package directions. Add the non-dairy topping to pudding and stir. Spoon pudding into clear party cups. Top with crushed cookies, so that it looks like dirt. Add gummy worms as a garnish.

For our family, meatloaf Monday is all about getting the family around the table for supper. A good way to start off the week is a plate of your favorite home-style comfort foods that are shared with the family. Meatloaf is one of our family favorites, especially served with a pile of creamy mashed potatoes, fried okra, and cream cheese spinach.

Back in the day, meatloaf was an inexpensive way for the housewives to stretch their meat dollars. Nowadays, choice ground beef can be nearly as expensive as a steak. So this menu dresses it up a bit. Served alongside a pile of creamy mashed potatoes, fried okra, and cream cheese spinach, this meal is a celebration on its own!

And the pound cake ending is surprisingly easy.

MEATLOAF MONDAY

Barbeque Meatloaf   172

Loaded Buttermilk Mashed Potatoes   174

Fried Okra   175

Tim's Favorite Pound Cake   176

Cream Cheese Spinach   177

Barbeque Meatloaf

When I met my husband Joe, meatloaf was one of the things that he could make, and it was delicious. This recipe is a combination of Joe's meatloaf recipe, which has celery stuffed with cheese in the middle, and my mama's recipe, which uses barbeque sauce. It's the ultimate meatloaf recipe. Y'all enjoy!

Makes 10–12 servings

Sauce:

1 (6-ounce) can tomato paste

1/2 cup ketchup

1/2 cup favorite barbeque sauce

1 teaspoon garlic powder

1 teaspoon onion powder

2 teaspoons Worcestershire sauce

2 eggs, whisked

1/2 teaspoon salt

1/2 teaspoon black pepper

Meatloaf:

3 pounds ground beef

1/2 cup rolled oats

1/2 cup dry bread crumbs

1 (5-ounce) bag seasoned croutons, crushed

2 medium onions, finely chopped

Stuffed Celery Filling:

4 (8-inch) ribs celery

4 (8-inch) strips Velveeta

Sauce for Topping:

1/2 cup ketchup

1/2 cup favorite barbeque sauce

Preheat the oven to 375 degrees.

Mix sauce ingredients in a bowl and set aside.

Using your hands, mix meatloaf ingredients together in a large bowl. Pour sauce into the meatloaf ingredients and combine well.

Place half of the mixture into a 9 x 12-inch baking pan. Stuff the cheese strips into the celery pieces and cut into 1-inch pieces. Take the pieces and make four 8-inch rows across the meatloaf. Cover with the remaining meat mixture. Mix together the topping sauce and spread it across the top of the meatloaf. Place in the oven and bake for 1 hour.

AUTUMN

Loaded Buttermilk Mashed Potatoes

Mashed potatoes is a staple dish that is served alongside many Southern favorites. If you have any left over, this is excellent reheated the next day.

8 medium Russet potatoes, peeled and cubed

1/2 cup (1 stick) butter

4 ounces cream cheese

2 teaspoons salt, or more

1 teaspoon black pepper, or more

1/2 cup buttermilk (more if needed)

In a large pan, boil potatoes in water until fork tender. Drain the potatoes. While potatoes are still hot, add the butter, cream cheese, and salt and pepper. Mash the potatoes, mixing all ingredients together. Add the buttermilk, and using a hand mixer, mix potatoes until creamy and smooth. (You may need a bit more buttermilk if potatoes are not creamy enough). Season to taste with additional salt and pepper.

Fried Okra

I always hated picking okra in the hot summertime because it was prickly and stickery. But I always loved eating the fried okra that Mutty would make. I would take in the basket of fresh okra and she would wash it, slice it up, and then fry it. Nothing better.

2 cups canola oil

2 cups washed and sliced okra

1 cup buttermilk

1 cup cornmeal

Salt

Heat the oil in a cast iron skillet on medium-high heat to about 375 degrees.

Meanwhile, place okra in a bowl with the buttermilk, then transfer okra to the cornmeal and dredge it.

Test the heat of the oil by dropping in a bit of corn meal. It should sizzle. Once oil is sizzling, add cornmeal-crusted okra, and fry until golden brown. Once done, remove okra and drain on a plate covered with paper towels. Season to taste with salt.

Tim's Favorite Pound Cake

Pound cakes have been passed down through generations of Southerners using the "cup of, cup of, cup of" recipe. In this case, it's measured by twos. The recipe is my friend Tim's, and it has turned out perfectly every time I've made it.

2 cups sugar

2 cups all-purpose flour

2 sticks (1 cup) butter

5 eggs

2 tablespoons vanilla extract

2 teaspoons almond extract

2 tablespoons bourbon

Pinch of salt

Preheat oven to 325 degrees. Using an electric mixer, mix all ingredients together well, divide between two greased and floured loaf pans, and bake for 1 hour. What could be easier?

Cream Cheese Spinach

When we were growing up, my little brother Chad was a bit weird. Not really, but when in elementary school, he loved spinach. He loved it so much that he would trade his dessert for spinach. How crazy is that? I like fresh spinach in salads or wilted, and my kids love this spinach with cream cheese. Now, I'm not saying that it will make you want to trade your dessert, but even if you don't like spinach, you might like it this way.

1/2 cup water

2 bunches fresh spinach, washed

4 ounces cream cheese

Salt and pepper

Heat water in a skillet on medium high and add fresh spinach. Cover the skillet with a lid and let the spinach wilt for a minute or two. Take lid off once the spinach is wilted and stir in cream cheese until combined. Season to taste with salt and pepper.

Winter

Chinese Non~Take~Out Dinner   183

The Night Before Christmas   187

*I*t's wintertime in the country. Time for the holidays, sparkly trimmings, and, of course, time to decorate and cook—my two favorite things. When it's cold outside, so all I want to do is cocoon. It is time for decking those halls and decorating every square inch of the house. The pecans that littered the ground a few months ago have been picked up and shelled, and are standing ready for a yummy pecan pie.

The kaleidoscope turns from orange plaid pillows to red plaids and black-and-white ticking. Pumpkins are traded out for old watering cans spilling out cuttings of fresh cedar that have been plucked from the woods. Red berries are sprinkled among the cedar and twinkling lights. Football is on the TV while I cook in the kitchen. The warmth from the oven feels good on a cold winter night.

This is the time of year that I wait for—when I can drag out my millions of vintage Christmas ornaments and prepare our favorite holiday foods. We have a pretty established menu for the holidays and one that our entire family anticipates every year. The food is as big a star of the holidays as the decorations and the presents are. It's funny how most of these dishes we only prepare at the holidays . . .

but they would be great anytime of year, especially the stuffed turkey breast.

CHINESE NON-TAKE-OUT DINNER

Orange Chicken   184

Fried Rice   185

Orange Chicken

One thing about living in the country is that we can't just run out for Chinese takeaway. So I make our favorite Chinese dishes at home. Our family relishes Orange Chicken and Fried Rice. It has just enough sweetness that we don't crave dessert afterwards. I serve it with steamed broccoli.

Marinade:

1 cup chicken broth

1/3 cup distilled white vinegar

1/4 cup teriyaki sauce

1/4 cup orange juice

1/4 teaspoon lemon juice

1/4 cup chopped Mandarin orange slices

1/2 cup juice from Mandarin oranges

1/2 cup tightly packed brown sugar

1/4 –1/2 teaspoon red pepper flakes

2 cloves garlic, minced

1/4 teaspoon grated fresh ginger

1/4 teaspoon black pepper

Chicken:

1 1/2 pounds boneless, skinless chicken breasts, cubed

2 cups all-purpose flour

1 cup canola oil

1 bag fresh broccoli florets

2 tablespoons cornstarch mixed with 1/2 cup hot water

1 green onion, chopped

For the marinade, mix all the ingredients together in a bowl. Pour 2/3 cup of the marinade into a ziplock plastic bag. Add the chicken and marinate in the refrigerator for 30 minutes.

Place the flour in a pan for dredging. Remove chicken from the bag, and roll in the flour. After dredging, heat oil in a large frying pan, then pan-fry the chicken until it is golden. Transfer chicken to paper towels to drain.

Sauté or steam the broccoli just until tender; drain.

Place the remaining marinade in a large skillet. Add cornstarch slurry and cook until it thickens to a sauce. Toss chicken and broccoli in the sauce and sprinkle with green onions.

Fried Rice

Fried rice is a perfect pairing with any Asian fare that you might be serving; or if you wanted to add some chicken, shrimp, or beef to this recipe, it could be a main dish meal. For those of us that do not have local Chinese take-out this is a great way to enjoy delicious Chinese food without leaving home

2 tablespoons canola oil

1 small onion, finely chopped

2 cloves garlic, minced

2 cups cooked white rice, cold

2 tablespoons soy sauce

2 tablespoons teriyaki sauce

1 small package frozen peas and carrots, thawed

2 eggs, beaten

Salt and pepper

2 green onions, chopped

Heat the oil in large nonstick skillet on medium heat. Add the onion and garlic and sauté until soft, stirring. Add the rice and heat until warm. Add soy sauce and teriyaki and mix into the rice. Add peas and carrots and stir in until heated. Push rice over to the side of the pan, leaving some space to cook the eggs. Add eggs to the skillet and stir rapidly until eggs are cooked, then stir into the rice mixture. Season to taste with salt and pepper. Transfer to a serving dish and sprinkle with green onion.

THE NIGHT BEFORE CHRISTMAS

Spicy Rosemary and Black Pepper Cashews   190

Layered Salad   193

Stuffed Turkey Breast   194

Holiday Dressing   196

Cranberry Relish   197

Jalapeño Corn Casserole   198

Sugar-Free Pecan Pie   201

*T*he night before Christmas is a pretty big night here at our country house. Everyone comes home for Christmas—my children who are living away, my parents, my brothers and their families—and we have a house full. Every bedroom is filled, every couch is taken, and there is excitement in the air. The smell of fresh pine and cedar drifts through the house, while lights twinkle from all of the banisters, mantels, and garlands. The main Christmas tree is always set up in the red room.

At the appointed time, we travel the half mile down our gravel road to our little church for a Christmas Eve service with our neighbors. Our church has 28 people attending most Sundays, but this night there will be standing room only. One of the things that I love most about this small town is the church. There are not any pretentious or snooty people here, just our neighbors who come dressed in overalls or work boots because that is who they are. As soon as you walk in the door, there is hugging and kissing and everyone there really wants to know how you are. The ladies are talking about what they're cooking, trading recipes, and finding out where Mary got her new boots. Then it's time to get down to business with the candlelight service. Afterwards, it's back out into the cold for the short drive home.

Pulling into the drive, the lights sparkle from every direction, and what once was an old wreck of a house now gleams with the beauty of Christmas. I am eager to get in there and get the food on the table in record time. The table is already set with the red transferware plates that come out for Christmas, along with the silver goblets that I got for a wedding present many years ago.

As I open the back door, the warmth and smells from inside radiate outside. The kids are hungry, and the anticipation for the meal trumps the packages under the tree. The Stuffed Turkey Breast is center stage. I put the corn casserole near Chad, because that is his favorite. As the blessing is finished, the plates begin swirling around the table and dinner is served.

"Merry Christmas to all."

Spicy Rosemary and Black Pepper Cashews

I always make these around the holidays. They make a great gift when put in a pretty bowl, wrapped in cellophane and tied with a beautiful bow. They are also good at any cocktail party or just for a yummy snack. We have rosemary year-round in the garden, so it is easy to go snip some rosemary and make this delicious recipe.

2 cups roasted cashews

1 tablespoon olive oil

1 tablespoon melted butter

1/2 teaspoon sea salt

1 teaspoon freshly cracked pepper

3 large sprigs rosemary, leaves only

Preheat oven to 350 degrees. Place nuts on a cookie sheet and drizzle with olive oil and melted butter. Sprinkle with salt, pepper, and rosemary. Mix all ingredients together, coating the nuts.

Bake until nuts are heated and sizzling. Remove from oven and cool.

WINTER

Layered Salad

My grandmother made this pretty layered salad, which she called President's Salad, every holiday. It looks gorgeous when served in a trifle dish or a large glass bowl. We have to be careful at our table, because my brothers have been known to scrape all of the toppings off of the salad, leaving the rest of us left with just lettuce. So you may want to mix just before serving. Or announce to your guests that it should be served by starting from the top and going all the way down to the bottom to get every layer.

1 head iceberg lettuce, chopped

1 (8~ounce) can sliced water chestnuts, drained

1 (12~ounce) bag frozen green peas, rinsed and drained

6 green onions, chopped

1 cup mayonnaise

1 cup shredded Colby Jack cheese

8 slices bacon, fried, drained, and chopped

1 green onion, chopped

Layer this salad beginning with the lettuce. Then add a single layer of water chestnuts. Next add green peas and then green onions. I open a fresh jar of mayonnaise that has not yet been refrigerated, as it spreads much better. Spread the mayonnaise across the peas carefully. Then top with cheese, bacon, and green onion. Refrigerate until serving.

Stuffed Turkey Breast

This is an amazing alternative to cooking an entire turkey, and when plated it looks very elegant. It is the best part of the turkey, in my opinion, with no bones to deal with. This recipe always makes up extra spinach filling that I just bake in a separate pan and serve as a side. In fact, there is enough filling to stuff two turkey breasts and still have extra. For our family, one boneless turkey breast is not enough for the holidays, as we have about fifteen people. It smells just wonderful!

1 (12-ounce) package bacon

1 cup chopped onion

2 eggs

1 cup ricotta cheese

1/2 cup (1 stick) butter, melted, divided

1 (28-ounce) bag chopped spinach, cooked in microwave and drained

3/4 teaspoon garlic powder

3/4 teaspoon dried oregano

1/2 teaspoon black pepper

2 (48-ounce) boneless turkey breasts

Preheat oven to 425 degrees. Cover a baking sheet with foil.

Fry the bacon then drain and chop. Cook the onions in 2 tablespoons bacon drippings until soft. Remove from pan.

In a bowl combine eggs, ricotta cheese, and 1/4 cup of the melted butter; mix together. Stir in the cooked spinach, bacon, onion, garlic powder, oregano, and pepper; mix thoroughly.

Cut the turkey breast in half lengthwise, so that there is a top and a bottom. Lay both halves flat on the baking sheet, cut side up. Spread a thick layer of spinach filling onto each half. Carefully place the top of the turkey breast onto the bottom turkey breast and use skewers to keep the two halves together with the filling inside. It is okay if a little of the mixture is spilling out. Pour remaining 1/4 cup butter over the top.

Repeat same steps for the second turkey breast. Bake for 40 minutes at 425 degrees. Lower heat to 350 degrees and bake 50 more minutes, until done.

Holiday Dressing

We always have cornbread dressing for Thanksgiving, so I like a little something different for other times. This is good any time of year and can be served with anything from Cornish hens to baked chicken breasts. This stuffing is full of sweet dried apricots and red-ripe apples mixed with savory sausage; it gives a great salty and sweet bite . . . it is sure to become a favorite.

2 boxes chicken-flavored stuffing mix

8 ounces ground sausage

1 onion, chopped

2 ribs celery, diced

8 dried apricots, chopped

1/2 cups chopped Red Delicious apple

1/2 cup chopped pecans

1 tablespoon poultry seasoning

Preheat oven to 350 degrees. Prepare a baking dish with nonstick spray.

Cook both boxes of stuffing according to package directions. Set aside.

Cook sausage and drain, reserving 2 tablespoons of drippings. Heat sausage drippings in a saucepan over medium heat. Add onion, celery, apricots, apple, pecans, and poultry seasoning, and cook until vegetables and fruit are softened.

In a bowl, mix together stuffing, sausage, and fruit/vegetable mixture to combine. Place in baking dish and bake until hot and golden on top.

Cranberry Relish

This is a wonderful, fresh alternative to a canned cranberry sauce. It is tart and sweet and has the delicious crunch of the chopped pecans. It is a great addition to any holiday table. 1 bag fresh cranberries

1 orange, peeled and seeded

1/2 cup pecans

1/2 cup sugar

Place all ingredients into a food processor and process until finely chopped. Serve chilled.

Jalapeño Corn Casserole

This is my former sister-in-law's dish that she brought every Christmas. Although she was not a fan of cooking, she made this one and it is absolutely decadent. It's spicy and cheesy corn deliciousness.

Makes 6–8 servings

1/2 cup (1 stick) butter, softened

8 ounces cream cheese, softened

2 cups shredded Colby Jack cheese, divided

4 pickled jalapeños, seeded and finely chopped

2 tablespoons jalapeño juice

1 (20-ounce) package frozen corn, thawed

Preheat oven to 350 degrees.

In a large bowl, stir together butter, cream cheese, and 1 cup of Colby Jack until well mixed. Stir in the chopped jalapeños and juice. Add the corn and mix until all ingredients are well incorporated. Place in 9 x 13-inch baking dish. Sprinkle the remaining cheese on top and bake until cheese is bubbly.

WINTER

Sugar-Free Pecan Pie

This wonderfully rich pecan pie has no added sugar but tastes rich and delicious. It is super easy to make, taking only a few minutes to whip together and get into the oven—but no one has to know.

1 prepared piecrust

4 eggs

2/3 cup Stevia, Splenda, or sugar substitute of your choice

1 1/4 cup Mrs. Butterworth's sugar-free syrup

1 cup chopped pecans

1/4 cup whole pecan pieces

Heat oven to 375 degrees. Line a pie pan with the piecrust.

In a large bowl, use a rotary mixer to beat the eggs, Stevia, and syrup together until mixed. Stop mixing, add the chopped pecans, and stir in. Pour filling into the pastry-lined pan. Place whole pecan pieces on the top of the pie in a decorative manner. Bake pie for 40 to 50 minutes, until filling is set and pastry is golden brown.

Variation: If you prefer a regular pecan pie with sugar, then just use the regular Mrs. Butterworth's syrup and use white granulated sugar in place of the sugar substitute.

FOOD FOR THOUGHT

Herb Bouquets

Everyone thinks of flower bouquets for their homes, but what about the beauty of a gathering of herbs. Mutty could be found any time of year gathering a bouquet for her Texas farmhouse. Sometimes it was a wildflower bouquet from the field or flowering branches from the trees or perhaps a handful of zinnias during the summer that she grew just for cutting. My mama has always done the same, and she has always planted an herb garden.

The herb garden sits just outside the perimeter of the playhouse and the chicken house and has practically every herb known to man. It was my mama's brilliant idea to start picking the herbs for making bouquets, which she would sprinkle around the house. These bouquets look lush and smell wonderful, and when they have spent their beauty, you can also use them in your cooking.

One of my favorite combinations is fresh rosemary, basil and lavender—it puts off a most permeating scent that infuses the entire house.

Just as everyone's home has its own style, it also has a smell that people recognize when they come through the door. When you live in a house that is over 150 years old, like we do, you want to make sure that the house always smells fresh. Herb bouquets are perfect for that.

All it takes to grow your own herbs are a few seeds and a few pots of dirt, then you are in business. Find your favorites and give your home a signature scent year-round.

Carolyn's Tips for Decorating Tables

Most people, when faced with the daunting task of decorating a party table, are not only stumped but stressed. A trip to the grocery store for a bouquet of flowers to be placed in a vase in the center of the table can be the extent of it.

Come on—you can do better than that, and it doesn't have to break the bank. How about decorating with your food, appetizers, juices, or wine? Your serving pieces make unique decorations too. You need all of these things anyway, so try arranging them to perfection. Your guests will be talking about your table for weeks to come.

In this case, trays are filled with utilitarian pieces that are not only practical but beautiful. Just as you would decorate any other space, it is important to have varied height on he tabletop, especially if you are serving buffet style. In that case, you can go as high as you want without having to worry about blocking the view. A buffet table is a great idea and I find much easier than having to pass heavy and hot entrée platters around the table. By stacking your plates and arranging silverware, entrées, and accoutrements all together, guests can easily get to what they need.

Cake stands are a fabulous way to show off just about anything, including biscuits or croissants for a morning brunch. They are also great for pies, cakes, and cookies, or, like I said, just about anything.

Another wonderful collectible is antique wooden cutting boards. They look marvelous on the tabletop and can hold just about anything—they are really handy as pedestals for the bread or biscuits. Here cheeses are kept soft under a cloche, and a glorious mix of olives is served in small glass compote. Beautifully baked breads filled with nuts and grains could be a centerpiece in itself atop this pretty, antique carved bread board.

A spooner is a magnificent vase for the crunchy breadsticks that will be used for dipping, or as a crunchy snack while sipping some wine.

Anyone who knows me knows of my passion for garden statuary. My husband is the poor soul who has had to carry it from the flea market to the car, probably one too many times. I simply cannot resist a crusty, painted urn or a beautiful statue, and I use them throughout the house. Here the urn is the centerpiece, surrounded with bluish-green hydrangeas that have just been cut from the garden. After picking the large heads of cabbage in our garden, it comes back in smaller heads, which I've mixed with the hydrangeas that I've picked as a beautiful addition to this floral centerpiece mixed with the hydrangeas.

I think of hydrangeas as my signature flower. The ones from the garden are much hardier because they are used to the elements. We have a plethora of colors: as the soil varies, so does the color of the blooms, and they come back year after year.

This utilitarian style of decorating is all about using what you have and using the pieces that you would serve with to create a gorgeous tablescape. I often cut branches for a centerpiece. For fall, a glorious arrangement can be made from branches with fall leaves and berries. Or sunflowers picked from the field can be surrounded by pumpkins.

In winter there are cedar branches, and red yaupon holly berries (do not eat!)

arranged in an old watering can for the table arrangement. Planting a flower garden from seed is inexpensive and allows you to have cut bouquets throughout much of the year.

A romance is born for me, seeing this delectable tabletop . . . food for thought.

INDEX

Almond-Crusted Salmon with Spring
    Greens and Blue Cheese, 124
Apples, Chocolate-Dipped, 168
Aunt Karen's Spaghetti, 111
Aunt Kim's Cheesy Spanish Rice, 42
Aunty Lou's Brisket, 86
avocado:
    Homemade Guacamole, 38
    Mexican Cole Slaw, 88
    Shrimp Ceviche, 36
Bacon-Jalapeño Cheesy Grits, 27
bacon:
    Aunt Kim's Cheesy Spanish Rice, 42
    Bacon-Jalapeño Cheesy Grits, 27
    Cheesy Scrambled Eggs Florentine, 24
    Cheesy Spinach and Orange Pepper
        Dip, 163
    Deviled Eggs, 89
    Layered Salad, 193
    Simply Perfect Shrimp BLT, 132
    Southern Mashed Potato Salad, 87
    Stuffed Turkey Breast, 194
Baloney and Egg Sandwich, Fried, 135
Barbeque Meatloaf, 172
Barbeque Ribs, Easy, 85
Bean Salad, Nana's, 165
beans:
    Black-Eyed Peas with Snaps, 59
    Nana's Bean Salad, 165
    White Chili with Chicken, 164
Beef Stew, Blue Ribbon, 150
beef, ground:
    Aunt Karen's Spaghetti, 111
    Barbeque Meatloaf, 172
    Carolyn's Best Lasagna, 102
    Carolyn's Easy Spaghetti Sauce, 110
    Nick's Cheeseburger in a Bowl
        Soup, 148
    Spicy Stuffed Cornbread, 44
    Venison Chili, 160
Beer Cheese Dip, Sherry's Famous, 98
Biscuits, Scratch Buttermilk, 20

Black-Eyed Peas with Snaps, 59
Blackberry Preserves, Texas Fencerow, 31
Blue Ribbon Beef Stew, 150
Brisket, Aunty Lou's, 86
Broccoli and Cheese Soup, 147
Buttermilk Biscuits, Scratch, 20
Buttermilk Mashed Potatoes, Loaded, 174
Caesar Salad with Homemade
    Dressing, 100
Cake, Coconut, 72
Cake, Grandmother's Fudge, 114
Cake, Strawberry Layer, 116
Cake, Tim's Favorite Pound, 176
Carolyn's Best Lasagna, 102
Carolyn's Easy Spaghetti Sauce, 110
Cashews, Spicy Rosemary and Black
    Pepper, 190
Catfish, Fried, 122
Celery, Pimento Cheese-Stuffed, 69
Ceviche, Shrimp, 36
Champagne Punch, Strawberry, 113
Cheese Dip, Sherry's Famous Beer, 98
Cheese-Stuffed Celery, Pimento, 69
cheese:
    Almond-Crusted Salmon with Spring
        Greens and Blue Cheese, 124
    Aunt Kim's Cheesy Spanish Rice, 42
    Bacon-Jalapeño Cheesy Grits, 27
    Caesar Salad with Homemade Dress-
        ing, 100
    Carolyn's Best Lasagna, 102
    Cheesy Spinach and Orange Pepper
        Dip, 163
    Cornbread, 55
    Cream Cheese Spinach, 177
    Family-Favorite Macaroni and
        Cheese, 56
    Fried Baloney and Egg Sandwich, 135
    Jalapeño Corn Casserole, 198
    Layered Salad, 193
    Loaded Buttermilk Mashed
        Potatoes, 174

Parmesan Garlic Toast, 112
Pasta with Garden-Fresh Tomato
    Sauce, 104
Pimento Cheese-Stuffed Celery, 69
Sherry's Famous Beer Cheese Dip, 98
Southwestern Squash Casserole, 45
Spicy Stuffed Cornbread, 44
Tomato, Cucumber, and Feta Salad, 60
Uncle Chad's Tomato Caprese Salad, 107
White Chili with Chicken, 164
Cheesy Grits, Bacon-Jalapeño, 27
Cheesy Scrambled Eggs Florentine, 24
Cheesy Spanish Rice, Aunt Kim's, 42
Cheesy Spinach and Orange Pepper Dip,
    123
Cherry Pie, Sugar-Free, 90
Chicken and Dumplings, Down-
    Home, 144
Chicken Pot Pie, 154
Chicken Salad, Cranberry, 66
Chicken, Nana's Famous Fried, 50
Chicken, Orange, 184
Chicken, White Chili with, 164
Chili with Chicken, White, 164
Chili, Venison, 160
Chocolate-Dipped Apples, 168
Chocolate Frosting, 115
Classic Cucumber Sandwiches, 70
Cobbler, Peach, 61
Coconut Cake, 72
Cole Slaw, 121
Cole Slaw, Mexican, 88
Corn Casserole, Jalapeño, 198
corn:
    Chicken Pot Pie, 154
    Cornbread, 55
    Jalapeño Corn Casserole, 198
    Mexican Cole Slaw, 88
    Spicy Stuffed Cornbread, 44
Cornbread, 55
Cornbread, Spicy Stuffed, 44
Country Sausage Gravy, 23

Cranberry Chicken Salad, 66

Cranberry Relish, 197

Cream Cheese Spinach, 177

Croutons, 101

Croutons, Hamburger Bun, 148

Cucumber Sandwiches, Classic, 70

Dad's Fish Dipping Sauce, 127

Deviled Eggs, 89

Dip, Cheesy Spinach and Orange
    Pepper 163

Double-Crust Piecrust, 93

Down-Home Chicken and Dumplings, 144

Dressing, Caesar Salad with
    Homemade, 100

Dressing, Holiday, 196

Dumplings, Down-Home Chicken and, 144

Easy Barbeque Ribs, 85

Eggs, Deviled, 89

Eggs Florentine, Cheesy Scrambled, 24

Family-Favorite Macaroni and Cheese, 56

Fish Dipping Sauce, Dad's, 127

fish:

    Almond-Crusted Salmon with Spring
        Greens and Blue Cheese, 124

    Fried Catfish, 122

    Southern Salmon Patties, 126

Fried Baloney and Egg Sandwich, 135

Fried Catfish, 122

Fried Okra, 175

Fried Rice, 185

Frosting, Chocolate, 115

Fudge Cake, Grandmother's, 114

Garlic Pickles, Spicy, 129

Garlic Toast, Parmesan, 112

Grandmother's Fudge Cake, 114

Gravy, Country Sausage, 23

Green Tomato Relish, 128

Grits, Bacon-Jalapeño Cheesy, 27

Guacamole, Homemade, 38

Gummy Worm Pudding Cups, 169

ham: Black-Eyed Peas with Snaps, 59

Hamburger Bun Croutons, 148

Holiday Dressing, 196

Homemade Guacamole, 38

Hush Puppies, 120

Jalapeño Corn Casserole, 198

jalapeño(s):

    Bacon-Jalapeño Cheesy Grits, 27

    Green Tomato Relish, 128

    Hush Puppies, 120

Jalapeño Corn Casserole, 198

Mexican Cole Slaw, 88

Nick's Favorite Fresh Salsa, 41

Shrimp Ceviche, 36

Spicy Stuffed Cornbread, 44

jam:

    Strawberry Preserves, 32

    Texas Fencerow Blackberry Preserves, 31

Lasagna, Carolyn's Best, 102

Layered Salad, 193

Lime Sherbet Punch, 71

Loaded Buttermilk Mashed Potatoes, 174

Macaroni and Cheese, Family-Favorite, 56

Meatloaf, Barbeque, 172

Mexican Cole Slaw, 88

Muffins, Texas Pecan Praline, 26

Nana's Bean Salad, 165

Nana's Famous Fried Chicken, 50

Nick's Cheeseburger in a Bowl Soup, 148

Nick's Favorite Fresh Salsa, 41

Okra, Fried, 175

Orange Chicken, 184

Parmesan Garlic Toast, 112

Pasta with Garden-Fresh Tomato Sauce, 104

pasta:

    Aunt Karen's Spaghetti, 111

    Carolyn's Best Lasagna, 102

    Carolyn's Easy Spaghetti Sauce, 110

    Macaroni and Cheese, Family-
        Favorite, 56

    Pasta with Garden-Fresh Tomato
        Sauce, 104

Peach Cobbler, 61

Peas with Snaps, Black-Eyed, 59

Pecan Pie, Sugar-Free, 201

Pecan Praline Muffins, Texas, 26

pecan(s):

    Chocolate-Dipped Apples, 168

    Chocolate Frosting, 115

    Cranberry Chicken Salad, 66

    Cranberry Relish, 197

    Holiday Dressing, 196

    Sugar-Free Pecan Pie, 201

    Texas Pecan Praline Muffins, 26;

Pickles, Spicy Garlic, 129

Pie, Chicken Pot, 154

Pie, Sugar-Free Cherry, 90

Pie, Sugar-Free Pecan, 201

Piecrust, Double-Crust, 93

Pimento Cheese-Stuffed Celery, 69

Potato Salad, Southern Mashed, 87

Potatoes, Loaded Buttermilk Mashed, 174

Preserves, Strawberry, 32

Pudding Cups, Gummy Worm, 169

Punch, Lime Sherbet, 71

Punch, Strawberry Champagne, 113

Relish, Cranberry, 197

Relish, Green Tomato, 128

Ribs, Easy Barbeque, 85

Rice, Aunt Kim's Cheesy Spanish, 42

Rice, Fried, 185

Rosemary and Black Pepper Cashews,
    Spicy, 190

Salad, Caesar, with Homemade
    Dressing, 100

Salad, Cranberry Chicken, 66

Salad, Layered, 193

Salad, Nana's Bean, 165

Salad, Southern Mashed Potato, 87

Salad, Tomato, Cucumber, and Feta, 60

Salad, Uncle Chad's Tomato Caprese, 107

Salmon Patties, Southern, 126

Salmon, with Spring Greens and Blue
    Cheese, Almond-Crusted 124

Salsa, Nick's Favorite Fresh, 41

Sandwich, Fried Baloney and Egg, 135

Sandwiches, Classic Cucumber, 70

Sauce, Dad's Fish Dipping, 127

Sausage Gravy, Country, 23

sausage:

    Carolyn's Best Lasagna, 102

    Carolyn's Easy Spaghetti Sauce, 110

    Cheesy Spinach and Orange Pepper
        Dip, 163

    Country Sausage Gravy, 23

    Holiday Dressing, 196

    Venison Chili, 160

Sherbet Punch, Lime, 71

Sherry's Famous Beer Cheese Dip, 98

Shrimp BLT, Simply Perfect, 132

Shrimp Ceviche, 36

Simply Perfect Shrimp BLT, 132

Soup, Broccoli and Cheese, 147

Soup, Nick's Cheeseburger in a Bowl, 148

Southern Mashed Potato Salad, 87

Southern Salmon Patties, 126

Southwestern Squash Casserole, 45

Spaghetti Sauce, Carolyn's Easy, 110

Spaghetti, Aunt Karen's, 111

Spicy Garlic Pickles, 129

Spicy Rosemary and Black Pepper Ca-
    shews, 190
Spicy Stuffed Cornbread, 44
Spinach, Cream Cheese, 177
spinach:
    Cheesy Scrambled Eggs Florentine, 24
    Cheesy Spinach and Orange Pepper
        Dip, 163
    Cream Cheese Spinach, 177
    Stuffed Turkey Breast, 194
Spring Greens and Blue Cheese, Al-
    mond-Crusted Salmon with, 124
Squash Casserole, Southwestern, 45
Stew, Blue Ribbon Beef, 150
Strawberry Champagne Punch, 113
Strawberry Layer Cake, 116
Strawberry Preserves, 32
Stuffed Turkey Breast, 194
Sugar-Free Cherry Pie, 90
Sugar-Free Pecan Pie, 201
Texas Fencerow Blackberry Preserves, 31
Texas Pecan Praline Muffins, 26
Texas's-Best Fried Green Tomatoes, 52
Tim's Favorite Pound Cake, 176
Toast, Parmesan Garlic, 112
Tomato Caprese Salad, Uncle Chad's, 107
Tomato, Cucumber, and Feta Salad, 60
Tomato Relish, Green, 128

Tomato Sauce, Pasta with Garden-
    Fresh, 104
Tomatoes, Texas's-Best Fried Green, 52
tomatoes:
    Aunt Kim's Cheesy Spanish Rice, 42
    Carolyn's Best Lasagna, 102
    Fried Baloney and Egg Sandwich, 135
    Green Tomato Relish, 128
    Homemade Guacamole, 38
    Mexican Cole Slaw, 88
    Nana's Bean Salad, 165
    Nick's Cheeseburger in a Bowl Soup, 148
    Nick's Favorite Fresh Salsa, 41
    Pasta with Garden-Fresh Tomato
        Sauce, 104
    Shrimp Ceviche, 36
    Simply Perfect Shrimp BLT, 132
    Texas's-Best Fried Green Tomatoes, 52
    Tomato, Cucumber, and Feta Salad, 60
    Uncle Chad's Tomato Caprese Salad, 107
    Venison Chili, 160
Turkey Breast, Stuffed, 194
Uncle Chad's Tomato Caprese Salad, 107
Venison Chili, 160
White Chili with Chicken, 164

METRIC CONVERSION CHART

VOLUME MEASUREMENTS		WEIGHT MEASUREMENTS		TEMPERATURE CONVERSION	
U.S.	Metric	U.S.	Metric	U.S.	Metric
1 teaspoon	5 ml	1/2 ounce	15 g	250	120
1 tablespoon	15 ml	1 ounce	30 g	300	150
1/4 cup	60 ml	3 ounces	85 g	325	160
1/3 cup	80 ml	4 ounces	115 g	350	175
1/2 cup	125 ml	8 ounces	225 g	375	190
2/3 cup	160 ml	12 ounces	340 g	400	200
3/4 cup	180 ml	1 pound	450 g	425	220
1 cup	250 ml	2 1/4 pounds	1 kg	450	230